DON'T BE YOURSELF

YOURSELF

Be a Better Person

Challenge your perspectives on dating and relationships

David Ross

ISBN: 0692637915
ISBN-13: 978-0692637913

Dedication

To mom and family.

Thanks for your love and support.

Table of Contents

Introduction

There is nothing noble in being superior to your fellow man; true nobility is being superior to your former self.

- Ernest Hemingway

I have planned many singles events - mixers, networking events, and speed dating events. Many people like speed dating because it allows you to have short "dates" (typically 5 minutes or less) with different people of the opposite sex. In most speed dating events, each person has a number. If you like someone, you write their number on a sheet of paper provided by the event organizers. At the end of the event, you return the paper with your likes to the event organizers. Typically, the person who you like will not know that you like them unless they like you. It's kind of like when a boy likes a girl, and he writes her a note that says "I like you if you like me. Do you like me?" Speed dating is the adult version of "I like you if you like me."

I recently organized a speed dating event and learned that five of my guy friends liked one of my good female friends - we will call her Rachel. I asked Rachel if any of my five guy friends ever approached her or asked her out and she said "No." I found it surprising that they never asked her out because we all lived in the Atlanta area, and we all attended some of the

9

same social events. They had several opportunities to ask her out, but they never did. I caught up with one of my guy friends a week later to find out why.

I asked him, "I noticed that you like Rachel. Did you ever approach her or ask her out?"

He replied, "No."

So I asked him, "Why not? She's friendly, she's down to earth, and she seems pretty approachable."

He replied, "I wasn't sure if she would be interested."

When he said that, another friend of ours who was listening to the conversation said, "Dude just be yourself." When I heard that suggestion, I remembered thinking that *being himself* was actually the problem.

We are often told to "Be yourself." This suggestion is sometimes vague, unhelpful, and counterproductive. It suggests that you are perfectly fine as you are, and you don't need to improve. This book will disrupt the "be yourself" mindset and hopefully change your perspective on dating and relationships. As you read, try not to fall into the trap of thinking that there are only two choices – 1) be yourself or 2) pretend to be someone else. This book presents a third option – 3) be a better person. This third option is critically important because, contrary to popular belief, women often don't want men to be themselves. Also, men often don't want women to be themselves. I've done many surveys and conducted many interviews to support that claim. I studied International Psychology, and I also work with people from different cultures. I enjoy listening and learning about people's dating and relationship experiences.

The Approach Impasse

I recently surveyed 150 men to find out why they don't approach women who they find attractive. I conducted the survey because women sometimes ask me "Why don't men approach? Are they shy?" There are various reasons men sometimes don't approach women, which I discuss in Chapter 6 - Why Men Don't Approach. Some men do not approach women who they find attractive because they are worried that the women will not be interested in them. These men have a condition known as *approach anxiety*. I discuss several ways to overcome *approach anxiety* in Chapter 8 - How to Overcome Approach Anxiety. For now, the point I am making is that men are being themselves when they don't approach.

I surveyed 225 women to find out why they are not interested in some men. The women in my survey said that they usually turned men down when they are genuinely not interested in them. I also asked the women "Why don't you initiate conversations with men you find interesting?" Most of the women said that, with regards to dating, they feel that the man should approach the woman and initiate the conversation.

Let's quickly recap. Women sometimes want men to approach them. Men sometimes don't approach because they are afraid that the woman might not be interested in them. Women sometimes don't approach men because they feel that the man should take the initiative and approach them. So basically, we have an impasse. Men and women often don't approach each other for reasons that amount to them being themselves. As a result, many potential relationships do not blossom. Instead, they become dreams and fantasies in the minds of timid individuals who did not seize the day.

The approach impasse highlights one of the key challenges in male and female interactions and relationships - men and women sometimes don't communicate well. Many married couples stress that communication is important. However, in dating scenarios, men and women sometimes don't clearly communicate what is important to them. If someone does not communicate well, it is not helpful to suggest that they be themselves. I discuss solutions to the approach impasse in Chapter 8 - How to Overcome Approach Anxiety. I also offer some communication tips in Chapter 9 - Good Communication.

The Hungry Don't Get Fed

Usually, by this point the vast majority of people see the flaw in saying "Be yourself" and instead, they say "Be authentic" or "Be genuine" or "Be your best self." These suggestions are better than saying "Be yourself" but they may not be the best suggestions for you. If you are struggling to get dates, or if you feel that it is taking too long to find that special someone, it is possible that you are authentic or genuine based on what you know. It is also possible that you may be a bit too eager to meet that special someone. Let me explain by introducing to you the concept that "The hungry don't get fed."

When you interact with someone for the first time, or you

are in the early stages of dating, you do not want to appear too eager, anxious, or hungry for affection – some refer to this behavior as being thirsty. For example, a guy may appear thirsty if he approaches a woman and the first thing out of his mouth is "Wow! You're really beautiful. You're amazing. I would love to take you out to dinner. Can I call you sometime?" This is a bad approach because it shows neediness and lack of confidence.

A woman may appear thirsty if she brings up marriage or talks about starting a family on a first date. Instead of discussing marriage on a first date it's better to get to know each other and learn as much as you can about each other. In real life (outside of the dating world) it's okay if you are hungry or thirsty. In the dating world, it looks bad. Be sure to read Chapter 7 - The Hungry Don't Get Fed - and take the Thirsty Test to make sure that you are not giving off thirsty vibes.

The Relationship Framework

If you wish to have healthy relationships, you should be aware of your strengths, limitations, values, and biases. You should also be aware of others' perspectives and views. As an international psychologist, whenever I interact with someone from a different culture, I am encouraged to do three things: [1]

1. Be aware of my values and biases.
2. Understand the worldview of my culturally different client.
3. Design the best therapy solution based on my understanding of myself and my client.

Interacting with the opposite sex is very similar to interacting with someone from a different culture – cultural sensitivity is important.

With cultural sensitivity in mind, the main goal of this book is to encourage you to follow the three steps of what I will refer to as the **relationship framework**:

1. Know yourself and invest in yourself so that you can be a better person.
2. Understand and appreciate the needs and perspectives of others (especially the opposite sex).
3. Think of the best interaction or relationship that makes sense for you and the other person.

Very few people can consistently apply this framework to their dating relationships. It requires an advanced level of self-awareness and understanding to consistently know yourself (your strengths and limitations), understand someone else's wants and needs, and interact with them in a healthy constructive way. Think about the second step of the relationship framework for a moment. If you are in a relationship (friendship, dating, or marriage) you should understand and appreciate the needs and perspectives of the other person. You also want the other person to understand your needs and perspectives on a regular basis. This understanding typically only happens if the person is in love with you, loves you consistently, or has a deep amount of respect for you.

Parents who love their children usually consistently think about their needs. Unfortunately, some parents don't provide a healthy amount of love. Also, some parents do not meet their children's emotional needs. I will touch on that in

Chapter 2 - Things Unsaid. Right now I am referring to parents who genuinely love their children and wish the best for them. Those parents tend to consistently think about their children's needs.

People who don't love you seldom think consistently about your needs or wants. Instead, they tend to focus on their specific needs and desires. They want what they like. If they had to choose between A) you being yourself and B) you doing something that they really like, they often prefer B) you doing something that they really like. Unfortunately, sometimes you don't know what they really like because they don't tell you. I've written this book to help you figure out what the opposite sex wants and likes.

Invest In Yourself

When you are in a relationship with someone, they often want you to be your best. "Be your best" in this context means that you are doing the best you can with what you have. Your potential (and future) dates often want you to be your best before the relationship begins. To be your best, you should consistently invest in yourself - specifically your mind and your body.

You should regularly invest in your mental well-being. Your brain is remarkably capable of changing and improving. There are many things that you can do to improve your brain or emotional health. To name a few - you can eat well, exercise regularly, sleep well, meditate, spend time in nature, and avoid stress. You can also improve your brain health by stimulating your mind. According to a *Psychology Today* article, [2] "One of the simplest things you can do to make your brain sweat is to try to understand points of views that you do not agree with. Open your mind and listen to arguments that make no sense to you — and try to find some sense in them." When you invest in your mental and emotional health, you will find it easier to tackle many of life's challenges.

You should also invest in your physical health and overall appearance. Your physical health and appearance are important for many reasons. When you invest in your physical health and overall appearance, you are more likely to have greater self-esteem and confidence. In the dating world, your physical health and appearance are important, because they are visible to others. In psychology, there is a term known as *thin slicing.* [3] Thin slicing refers to the fact that people make decisions about you within seconds of meeting you. The term thin slice comes from the fact that you don't have to eat an entire cake or pie to know how it tastes. You can simply have a thin slice.

People take "thin slices" of information about you and draw larger conclusions. For example, if you are well-dressed and well-groomed many people will assume that you are successful. If you have a nice physical appearance people will assume that you are healthy and fun. Your appearance is one of the four key elements of sex appeal - which I discuss in Chapter 5 - Sex Appeal.

When you invest in yourself and constantly try to improve you will find the dating process a lot easier and rewarding. Don't make the mistake of assuming that you are perfectly fine, and everyone else is the issue. There is a saying that "Happiness is not only about finding the right person it is also about being the right person." My wish is for you to be the right person - a more knowledgeable person - a better person.

CHAPTER 1

When to Be Yourself

A year from now you will wish you had started today.

- Karen Lamb

The Dating IQ Quiz

The first step of the relationship framework is to know yourself and invest in yourself so that you can be a better person. Let's see what you know about dating by testing your dating IQ with a short five question multiple choice quiz. These questions apply to dating and relationship scenarios involving adults. There are no wrong answers. There are simply good answers and better answers. The best answer is based on the majority of responses to a survey or a study. You will get points for each question answered. Please note that this is not a scientific IQ test - it is mainly for discussion purposes.

Answer all questions and only select **one answer** for each question. You should write your answer on a sheet of paper or save it on your phone / mobile device. One last thing – the "It depends" option means that it depends on the context or scenario.

1. Do men like women who they perceive as more intelligent than themselves?

   A. Yes

   B. No

   C. It depends

2. Do women like nice guys?

   A. Yes

   B. No

   C. It depends

3. If a man and a woman are on a first date, who should pay?

   A. They should go Dutch - split the bill

   B. The woman should pay

   C. The man should pay

4. Who lies more - men or women?

   A. Men

   B. Women

   C. It depends

5. If a man and a woman see each other for the first time, and they both like each other, who should approach who?

A. The man should approach the woman

B. The woman should approach the man

C. It depends

Thanks for taking the quiz. We will go over your results in a little bit.

When To Be Yourself

You have many important positive qualities. You should keep and maintain your positive qualities. For example, if you are professional, organized, reliable, trustworthy, or punctual you should continue to have those qualities. Many people rely on your positive qualities, even if they don't tell you that they do. When I say "be a better person" I am suggesting that you add to your good qualities and remove the bad qualities. You being a better person is analogous to a software upgrade.

When you upgrade your computer or phone operating system, you typically want to keep the features that you like. You want to add new features to the features that work well for you. You also want to fix bugs and issues that may prevent you from achieving your goals. When being yourself gets you positive results then be yourself. When being yourself does not get you the results that you want it may be time for a self-upgrade.

When Not To Be Yourself

Sometimes when you love (or really like) someone, you will do things that you don't normally do or try things that you don't know how to do. For example, if you love someone who likes to travel, but you don't travel much, you might consider traveling a little more. Or if you like someone who loves to dance, but you don't know how to dance, you might consider taking dance lessons. That is the essence of not being yourself - learning new things, going new places, and as a result, becoming a better person.

Your willingness to learn new things can also be applied to other abilities - such as your ability to communicate and listen. You can strengthen your relationships (friendships, dating, marriage, etc.) by improving your communication skills. You can learn to do many things that you don't presently do. Throughout this book, I will highlight the importance of learning new things - new things about yourself and new things about the opposite sex.

Learning about yourself is important because sometimes you have bad habits that you are unaware of. Many men and women have bad habits that they are unaware of. The good news is that you can get rid of your bad habits once you identify them. Here are some common bad habits that are sometimes not addressed in dating and also in non-dating scenarios:

1. **Bad posture or poor body language:** If you have bad posture your body language might suggest that you have low self-esteem. You should consider engaging in activities and behaviors that promote good posture such as martial arts, yoga, dance, athletics, or exercise. Good posture is attractive to most people because it suggests that you are confident and perhaps competent.

21

2. **Neediness or anxiousness:** There is a fine line between being intentional/persistent and being needy or thirsty. Men and women sometimes give off thirsty vibes during their interactions. Be sure to read Chapter 7 - The Hungry Don't Get Fed - and take the Thirsty Test to make sure that you are not giving off thirsty vibes.

3. **Poor eye contact:** If you have difficulty making eye contact, some people may feel that you lack confidence. Men who have difficulty making eye contact are sometimes perceived as untrustworthy. Practice making eye contact. Keep in mind that your eye contact should not be a constant stare. A good rule of thumb is that during a conversation you should try to make eye contact 60 to 70 percent of the time.

4. **Poor communication skills:** Many people have challenges communicating clearly because they don't want to say the wrong thing. Communication habits are usually influenced by childhood or family dynamics. Whatever the cause may be, no one likes bad communication. Be sure to read Chapter 9 - Good Communication - to learn some helpful tips.

Men and women often don't tell you what you can improve upon. They also sometimes don't share their likes and dislikes. Instead, they say things like "Be yourself," which suggests that dating should be easy. Dating will be easy if you know the rules, you know the expectations, and you have experience socializing. Most sports and activities are easy if you know the rules, you know the expectations, and you have experience playing. For example, if you know how to play tennis, and you know the rules of tennis, then tennis is probably easy for you. If you know how to cook, and you have a lot of experience cooking, then cooking is probably easy for you. If you have been working at your job for a long time, your job is probably easy for you because you know what needs to be done and how to do it.

To be fair to the men and women who don't communicate their likes and dislikes - sometimes they don't share their likes or dislikes because they don't know if you can handle that information. For example, you have probably been in awkward situations where someone likes you romantically, and you don't like them because you are not attracted to them. Understandably, you are not comfortable telling them that you are not attracted to them. If you tell them that you are not attracted to them, it might come across as mean or insensitive. You're not a mean or insensitive person. You're simply not romantically interested in them.

It is perfectly okay that you cannot explain to someone why you don't like them. You don't have to explain - that's my job. That is one of the reasons I've written this book. I want men and women to think about each other's perspectives, wants, and desires. With that in mind, let's take a look at your quiz results.

Dating IQ Quiz Answers

I like to keep things simple. The best answer to each question is C. If you chose A or B as the answer you get 10 points for that specific question. If you chose C, you get 20 points for that question. Here is an explanation of the best answers:

Question 1: Do men like women who they perceive as more

intelligent than themselves?
Answer: *It depends.*

It depends on how you define like and how you define intelligent. Recent studies [4] have shown that men like intelligent women as friends but they may not want to date them. So basically men like intelligent women but they may not initially like them in a romantic way. The good news is that if someone likes you as a friend you may have an opportunity to set a foundation for a more serious relationship. Don't dismiss a good friendship opportunity. There is a saying that *friendship leads to love but love never leads to friendship - Lord Byron.*

It also depends on how you define intelligent. If your house needs plumbing and you are not a plumber, then a licensed plumber is more intelligent than you are with regards to plumbing. If you need a website, and you know nothing about designing or building websites, then an experienced website developer is more intelligent than you are with regards to building websites. Whether you are a man or a woman, always appreciate and respect other's skills and abilities - you will go very far in life if you do.

Question 2: Do women like nice guys?
Answer: *It depends.*

It depends on your definition of like. It is true that women like nice guys. The problem is that they sometimes don't like the nice guys the way the nice guys want to be liked. There are many studies [5] [6] [7] that say that women who are looking for short-term fun don't want nice guys. Nice guys are often considered boring and predictable. Women who want long-term relationships are more likely to date nice guys but they still hope for some of the "bad boy" qualities. I will elaborate more on this in Chapter 3 - Women's Wants.

Men, on the other hand, are okay with dating nice women. [8] If a man is attracted to a woman she will not lose points for being nice - she will most likely gain points. Men like women who are understanding, or empathetic, or both. Those qualities are consistent with being nice. When you add nice to nice-looking, you have a winning combination. I will elaborate more on this in Chapter 4 - Men's Wants.

Question 3: If a man and a woman are on a first date who should pay?
Answer: *The man should pay.*

According to a survey [9] by the advertising agency Leo Burnett, 68 percent of men pay on the first date. Another survey showed that a larger percentage of men -75 percent - expect to pay on the first date. If you know a guy who is unsure about who should pay on a first date, please recommend this book to him. Even in today's society, many women feel that a man has two very important roles - protect and provide. As a result, a man should be willing to pay on the first date. I will elaborate more on this in Chapter 3 - Women's Wants.

Note to men: Many women are very independent and provide for themselves because the men in their lives did not meet those roles. Most of these women welcome a confident man who can protect and provide. As a result, they don't mind if a man pays. On the first couple of dates, you should expect to pay. If money is an issue, then creativity is your friend. There are many fun and inexpensive activities. Thanks to the Internet and mobile devices they are all at your fingertips. Be sure to read Chapter 3 - Women's Wants.

Question 4: Who lies more men or women?
Answer: *It depends.*

This one is tricky because there are studies that say women lie more while other studies say men lie more. The discrepancy has to do with the fact that there are lies, and there are white lies. White lies are considered harmless lies. Both men and women tell white lies quite often. For example, if someone likes you but you don't like them it's easy to say that you are in a relationship already or that you are taking a break from dating. Those types of lies are totally understandable but not necessary. Chapter 9 talks about good communication. If you communicate well, you won't need to lie.

Question 5: If a man and a woman see each other for the first time and they both like each other, who should approach whom? **Answer:** *It depends.*

It depends on how you view or define "approach". Striking up a casual conversation or making a simple observation can be considered an approach. With this in mind, either person can approach the other. Women should consider initiating conversations because some men are introverts and usually don't approach women. To be clear - do not confuse introversion with fear of talking to women. There is a character on the TV sitcom *The Big Bang Theory*, who is terrified of speaking to women unless he is drunk. This condition is known as *selective mutism*.

Introverts are comfortable having conversations with women. They sometimes don't initiate conversations with women simply because they feel that approaching a woman (or anyone) out of the blue would be impolite or an intrusion on their day. Introverts tend to be pretty laid back and take comfort in observing the world around them. They are usually deep thinkers. I will elaborate on how to appeal to introverts in Chapter 4.

Dating IQ Quiz Scores

Your score should be between 50 and 100 points. If your score is not between 50 and 100 points, please re-calculate your total score. Remember that you get 10 points for the question if you chose A or B, and you get 20 points if you chose C. Here is the score breakdown:

i. **90 to 100 points:** You have an impressive dating IQ. Many people can learn from you if they are ready to receive your knowledge. If you are single at the moment, you most likely won't be single for long. There are many people who you can connect with. Your dating aptitude combined with this book will enable you to make the right investments in yourself and connect with a special person. If you have not already met that special someone, you will meet them soon.

ii. **70 to 80 points:** You have a very good dating IQ. You have had opportunities to connect with special people, and you will have more opportunities to connect with special people. This book will help you capitalize on future opportunities. If you are single at the moment don't worry - the single life is not for you. When the timing is right, you will connect with someone special.

iii.   **50 to 60 points:** You have a lot of potential. You can realize your potential by embracing other perspectives. Try not to expect too much too soon. You can become a great partner for someone if you develop a friendship first. Remember that friendship leads to love but love never leads to friendship.

iv.   **Less than 50 points:** You most likely did not answer all of the questions. Or perhaps you made a mistake somewhere. If you answered all of the questions, you should not have less than 50 points. You should re-tally you score.

Chapter Summary

You probably noticed that most of the quiz answers were "It depends." The frequency of "It depends" shows that when interacting or dating you should try to be flexible and aware of contexts. Things are often not clear-cut – and that is a good thing. For example, some women say that they want a tall guy, but they date or marry a short guy. Sometimes, it's because the short guy is confident and funny. Men with no kids sometimes say they don't want a woman with kids, but then they meet a single mom and marry her. Sometimes, it's because that single mom is down to earth and selfless. Children help you become selfless because they often make you focus on someone other than yourself.

The quiz questions highlight some areas where you can be a better person as opposed to simply being yourself. For example, if you are very intelligent you don't want to come across as a know it all who does not appreciate what others bring to the table. Try to appreciate other people's skills and talents - you might need them someday. Also, if you are a nice guy make sure you are not a boring, predictable nice guy. Think about great movies - they often involve intrigue, surprises, mystery, or suspense - and women like these things. This is one of the reasons men should approach. A positive approach is a pleasant surprise - it can make a woman's day.

Women sometimes wonder if it is okay for them to approach a guy. My answer to that question is yes. In an ideal world, the man would approach and charm the woman and have her smiling and laughing. They would then exchange numbers and keep in touch and either have fun times or develop a wonderful relationship. Unfortunately, we don't live in an ideal world.

Sometimes men don't approach because they are focused on something other than approaching. For example, if a man is shopping for tools or electronics he may be focused on finding that tool or electronic product. Also, if a man is preoccupied (working at an event, DJing, playing in a band, taking pictures, etc.), he may not approach because if the approach does not go well, it could negatively affect his ability to focus. Also, if a man has a lot going on (work, projects, school, family, etc.), he may not have a lot of time to date. If he does not have a lot of time to date, then he is less likely to approach. I discuss various reasons that men don't approach in more detail in Chapter 6.

Step 1 of the relationship framework is to know yourself and invest in yourself so that you can be a better person. By reading this book, you are making an important investment in yourself because you are learning new things. Step 2 of the relationship framework is to understand and appreciate the needs and perspectives of others (especially the opposite sex). When you appreciate the perspectives of others, you stimulate your mind - which improves your brain. Remember that *Psychology Today* article I mentioned in the introduction: [2] "One of the simplest things you can do to make your brain sweat is to try to understand points of views that you do not agree with. Open your mind and listen to arguments that make no sense to you—and try to find some sense in them." Learning new things and learning about others are key ingredients that can help you with step 3 of the relationship framework - think of the best interaction or relationship that makes sense for you and the other person.

Chapter 2

Things Unsaid

*The most important thing in communication is hearing
what isn't said.*

- Peter Drucker

Good Connections

Friendships, dating relationships, and marriages work really
well when the people involved have a good connection. There
are many different ways to connect. You can connect on a
physical level, an emotional level, an intellectual level, or a
spiritual level. Your level of connection depends on what you
feel is important to you. Here are some examples of ways to
connect on the various levels mentioned:

1. **Physical connections:** A good physical connection exists
   when you and your partner (or person of interest) like
   each other's physical qualities and appearance. In this
   case, physical qualities refer to anything that appeals to
   the five senses - sight, hearing, taste, smell, and touch.
   For example, if you and your partner like how each other
   looks, smells, and feels, then you have a good physical
   connection.

2. **Emotional connections:** A good emotional connection exists when you and your partner understand each other and feel safe sharing your deepest feelings with each other. Here are some key ingredients of a good emotional connection:

   a) You both feel comfortable being vulnerable or emotionally "exposed."

   b) You both understand each other's peculiarities and personality quirks.

   c) You have a similar sense of humor - you can laugh or appreciate each other's jokes.

   d) You both communicate respectfully with each other. You can disagree without being disagreeable.

   e) You both respect and appreciate each other, and you don't try to change each other.

3. **Intellectual connections:** If you have similar ideas and similar world views than you have a good foundation for an intellectual connection. Also, if you appreciate each other's hobbies or passions, you have a good foundation for an intellectual connection. An intellectual connection does not require both of you to have the same level of education. For example, if you are a lawyer or a doctor who likes to cook, you can appreciate someone (with no degree) who also likes to cook. If that person happens to be a good chef or a business owner, you can both enjoy and enhance each other's culinary skills. When you combine your intellectual connection with an emotional connection, a great relationship can blossom.

4. **Spiritual connections:** Spiritual connections happen when you and your partner respect and appreciate each

other's beliefs and share the same core values. For example, if you and your partner have the same religious beliefs you are likely to connect on a spiritual level. Also, if you both attend the same church (or similar churches), you can connect on a spiritual level because you can share stories about your church experiences.

This chapter will focus on some of the steps required to form a good emotional or intellectual connection. Chapter 5 - Sex Appeal - will address some of the requirements for a good physical connection. Chapter 10 - Spirituality and Self - will address some of the requirements for a good spiritual connection.

Good connections require good communication. Unfortunately, sometimes it is not easy to discuss relevant topics or share your concerns. Sometimes there are things that you don't want to discuss in the early stages of a relationship. Your reservations make sense because you want to be sure that you can trust someone before you share things about yourself. It goes both ways - some people don't discuss things with you because they want to feel that they can trust you. If you notice that someone does not want to talk about something, don't press the issue. You can acknowledge that you noticed that they don't want to discuss the issue. Just don't try to push them to discuss the issue unless you feel that it is critically important or time sensitive.

Ten topics that are not sufficiently discussed in adult relationships

Things that are unsaid are sometimes more interesting than things that are said. I surveyed and interviewed 120 women and 102 men to find out what they felt are important things that should be discussed in relationships. The results led to my list of the ten things that are not sufficiently discussed in adult relationships. The list will start with number ten - similar to David Letterman's Top Ten list.

Number 10 - Fears

Franklin D. Roosevelt said, "The only thing we have to fear is fear itself." Some men and women did not get the memo. When it comes to relationships and communication, men and women are sometimes afraid to discuss their fears. Men are pressured to appear brave and tough. As a result, they are sometimes afraid to talk to women (and other men) about things they fear. This fear of fears presents you with an opportunity. If someone feels that they can discuss their fears with you, then you will have an easier time connecting with them.

Fears are not limited to things like snakes, spiders, insects, or critters. Men and women are sometimes afraid of talking about their finances or employment because they are not where they want to be. Men and women are also sometimes uncomfortable talking about previous relationships, health, family dynamics, or childhood experiences.

Recommendations: Conversations about fears or concerns can be tough sometimes. Fortunately, there are many helpful tips for having tough conversations. [10] [11] The steps in the relationship framework outlined in the introduction can be applied to conversations about fears. The relationship framework recommends that you know yourself, know the other person, and decide what type of interaction or relationship is best. With regards to things unsaid, you should know your views, know the other person's views, and then use the information to strengthen your relationship. For example, if someone is not comfortable talking about their last relationship, you can start the conversation by sharing something about your last relationship and then asking about theirs. When you both share information with each other, you will probably have a stronger relationship. Make sure that the other person feels safe and appreciated when they share their fears or concerns with you.

If you feel that someone has a fear that prevents them from living a normal life, try to be supportive or encouraging. Sometimes motivational or inspirational messages can help. If that does not work, recommend that they talk to someone about their fears. Fears and phobias are very common and can be treated. Mental health professionals such as psychologists, psychiatrists, licensed therapists or counselors are very capable of helping people overcome their fears. Also, many health insurance plans cover various forms of mental health therapy.

Number 9 - Health

It is sometimes not easy to talk about health issues. For example, if someone had surgery to remove a mass they may not volunteer that information. People are sometimes private about health challenges that they have - especially if those health challenges are not obvious. If the health-related issue is obvious, then you may be able to ask questions about it. Keep in mind that if you have questions about someone's health make sure that they feel they can trust you with the answer. If they don't feel comfortable sharing health information with you, then acknowledge their right to privacy and let them know that it's okay.

Recommendations: Sympathy is important when discussing health related issues. Empathy is also helpful. There are some things that you are not comfortable discussing so be respectful of others' wishes. If you feel that someone is not comfortable talking about a health issue, you can start the conversation by sharing a health issue that you are comfortable sharing. After you share, you can ask about their health related issue.

Number 8 - Political or world views

Politics can be a third rail in some interactions or relationship. If you understand the comparison, please oblige me while I explain to my unfamiliar readers. Train tracks used by many mass transit systems (such as the New York City subway) have three rails. Two rails are for the train's wheels, and a third rail (next to the two rails or in the middle) provides electricity to the train. Trains require a lot of electricity. Therefore, the third rail carries a substantial amount of electrical current. If you touch the third rail, you will be shocked to death. Track workers and anyone near the train tracks know to avoid the third rail.

Thanks to the divisive nature of much of politics, some politicians and political issues are very controversial. As a result, you should avoid discussing politics in most non-political settings unless you feel that it is safe to do so. For example, if you are in a setting where most people share similar political views it may be okay to discuss the topic of the day. If you are dating someone who has strong political views that differ from your political views, then you should proceed with caution. Don't make assumptions about the reasons for their political views. Instead, ask questions to understand why they have their political views.

It is helpful to know how someone views the world and whether or not they feel that they can contribute to a better world. When possible, you should discuss some of the global (and local) challenges and crises even if you cannot do anything specific to help. Sometimes discussions about how to help can lead to helpful actions. For example, you can discuss a natural disaster with a friend or a group of friends and challenge yourselves to do something helpful. Your discussion may lead to a donation or some other helpful action.

Recommendations: If you are dating someone who has similar political views then you may have an easy opportunity to connect. This point of view is supported by an old proverb that says *"The enemy of my enemy is my friend."* People like when you have similar views to theirs. [12] It makes them feel that you have a shared bond, which helps you connect. [13]

You can also connect if you and the other person have different political views. If you are patient and understanding while someone shares their views, you will come across as a reasonable, confident person. Reasonableness and confidence are two very attractive qualities in a man or woman. Remember that step two of the relationship framework is to appreciate the other person's perspective.

Number 7 - Family

Sadly, some families are dysfunctional or filled with drama. As a result, some people minimize their interaction with family or specific family members. If you had a dysfunctional family, you might sometimes avoid them because you don't want to deal with drama or chaos. You may see the chaos as a pit seeking to suck you in. What you may not realize is that if you succeeded in spite of the dysfunction in your family the chaos was not a pit - it was a ladder. You climbed the ladder to success and as a result, you are wiser and more capable. Your mission, if you choose to accept it, is to enlighten and encourage others with your experiences. You can help others succeed when they learn from your success.

Recommendations: Dysfunctional families can be emotionally draining. If you are aware of someone's family challenges you should try to be understanding and empathetic. No family is perfect. You probably have challenges with some family members - everyone does. As a result, you should make the other person feel that it is safe to talk to you about their family challenges. You can start the conversation by sharing a story about your family. The more you share with them, the more likely they are to share with you.

Number 6 - Love

Everyone needs a certain amount of love. Unfortunately, many people have not received the necessary amount of love needed to function in an emotionally healthy way. For example, some children are raised in less than ideal or dysfunctional homes - homes where they did not receive the necessary amount of love needed to function in an emotionally healthy way. As a result, they may need more love than "average" from a relationship. Your goal should be to determine whether or not you can provide the necessary levels of love needed.

Recommendations: Here are some simple ways to determine how much love your partner may need in a relationship:

a) There is a great book entitled *The Five Love Languages*. [14] Identify your love languages and their love languages. When you know what makes someone feel loved you will have an easier time connecting with them.

b) Find out if they feel loved in general. Do they have a loving relationship with family or friends? If they have a loving relationship with family or friends they are more likely to have reasonable expectations regarding love.

c) If you can - try to find out if they received love during childhood or adolescence. Discussions about childhood may be a delicate topic in some cases so be careful and patient. It may help if you start out by sharing some of your childhood or adolescent experiences.

d) If you feel that they want more love than you can give, then do not let things go too far. Be honest with yourself and with them. Comment on their good qualities and let them know that you don't feel that you are the one for them. You can say something along the lines of "I appreciate ____ about you, but I don't feel that I am the one for you" or "You're a great person, but I don't think we are a good fit. Are you okay with us being friends?"

Number 5 - Sex

Sexual desires are often not discussed in great detail because of societal pressures to be politically correct or religious pressure to appear "moral." Women are pressured to appear chaste or not slutty. As a result, women are less likely to initiate conversations about sex. Men sometimes don't initiate conversations about sex for various reasons. For example, some men feel that it is not a gentlemanly thing to do. Other men are not sure what to say and don't want to risk coming across as creepy or horny. Here are some of the common reasons men and women don't discuss sex:

a) Their parents never discussed sex with them, so they don't know how to have a conversation about sex.

b) They feel that it is not politically correct to talk about sex because they are often in environments where sex is not discussed.

c) They were raised in conservative or religious environments that discourage sex before marriage - which sometimes also discourages conversations about sex.

Recommendations: Make it safe to discuss anything and everything. If you don't feel disrespected by someone's views, allow them to share their views. Some people don't talk to you about sex because they don't know if you will accept their views. They may worry that you will judge them. To avoid this problem, let them know that you don't like to judge.

Sometimes conversations about sex flow more smoothly when you initiate. If you share your views about sex or sexuality in a polite, respectful manner, it will be easier for the other person to follow your lead and share as well. You can learn a lot about someone's intimate likes when you have a healthy discussion about sex or intimacy.

Number 4 - Trauma

Some people have experienced stressful events that caused emotional or psychological trauma. These types of events are often unexpected, and the person victimized typically had no control over what happened or felt powerless to stop it. Some examples of potentially traumatic events are as follows:

a) **Crime or community violence:** People who live in high-crime neighborhoods are sometimes victims of crimes such as robbery, burglary, or vandalism. These victims sometimes feel traumatized by the crime they experienced.

b) **Domestic violence:** Physical or sexual violence between intimate partners can be traumatizing. The violence can be implied via a threat; it does not have to actually happen.

41

c) **Sexual assault:** According to the Rape, Abuse and Incest National Network (RAINN) 1 out of every 6 American women have been the victim of an attempted or completed rape in her lifetime. Also, 10 percent of rape victims are men.

d) **War-related violence:** Mental and emotional well-being are sometimes casualties of war. Soldiers and victims of war sometimes experience traumatic events during war. As a result, they suffer from post-traumatic stress disorder (PTSD).

e) **Medical trauma:** Some people are traumatized by life-altering surgery or a life-altering medical diagnosis. For example, a person may feel traumatized if they are told that they have diabetes or some other medical condition.

f) **Natural disaster:** A natural disaster is typically a catastrophic event such as a hurricane, tornado, or earthquake. Natural disasters often cause significant damage to property and sometimes cause death. These disasters can be traumatizing to some.

g) **Childhood trauma:** Childhood trauma and related issues are so significant they deserve a separate category. We will discuss childhood issues in a bit.

Recommendations: Empathy is key. If you know someone who experienced a traumatic event be sympathetic and understanding. Consider saying something along the lines of "I'm sorry to hear about that. Thank goodness you made it through." Saying "I'm sorry to hear that" or "I'm sorry that happened to you" is an effective way to show empathy.

Psychologists refer to this "apology" as a *superfluous apology*. [12] In this context you are not accepting blame, you are simply showing regret. You are letting the other person know that you understand their experience, and you wish things had turned out better.

Number 3 - Communication

Many couples who have been married for a long time (20 years or more) say that communication is very important. The fact that communication is so important in marriage suggests that if you are dating and wish to be married, then you should communicate well. Also, if you are simply getting to know someone and hope to date them in the future, then you should communicate well. If you think about it, you should communicate well as often as you can. Why wait until you're married? By then it may be too late. See Chapter 9 for communication tips.

Recommendations: One way to know if you are communicating well is to ask others if you communicate well. Start with a trusted friend or family member and ask them if they feel that you communicate well. In general, it is a good idea to check in with trusted friends or family members and find out if there are any areas that they feel you should work on. Make sure that they understand that you are asking because you want to improve as a person.

Another way to know if you are communicating well is to pay attention to the results of your communication. If people tend to be bothered, stressed, or frustrated when you speak to them, it is possible that you are not communicating well. Also, if people tend to avoid having extended conversations with you, it is possible that you are not communicating well. If on the other hand, people react in a positive manner when you speak to them then it is possible that you are communicating well. For example, if people smile or laugh when you talk to them it suggests that you are connecting with them. Also, if people are comfortable talking to you and listening to you, it suggests that you are connecting with them.

Number 2 - Money

Mark Twain said that *"The lack of money is the root of all evil."* I would not go quite that far. I will simply say that lack of money causes problems. Here are some problems caused by lack of money:

a) Women with little or no money sometimes want a man with money. These women like having a sugar daddy to help them with their financial needs.

b) Men with little or no money sometimes want a woman with money. Those men want a sugar mommy.

c) Men who have money sometimes shy away from women with little or no money because they feel the women may be gold diggers.

d) Society sometimes pressures women to date men who make more money than them.

e) Women who have money sometimes avoid men with little or no money because some men feel resentful if their partner makes significantly more money than them.

f) Men with little or no money sometimes shy away from women with money because they feel the woman may be too high maintenance.

When lack of money is not the issue there are other potential issues. Some women feel that a man who desires them should spare no expense. Men on the other hand often don't want to spend too much money too soon. This concern sometimes factors into a man's decision about approaching a woman - especially in online dating scenarios. Women sometimes say that they want a man who loves to travel. Generally speaking, men who can afford to travel and don't travel feel that traveling is too expensive, or they don't feel that it is worth it.

There are many single men with one or more houses, two or more degrees, and good jobs who don't travel much. They can certainly afford to travel because getting a college degree or buying house is a lot more difficult than taking a trip. These men are more likely to travel with the person they are dating if they feel that the trip is not all about them spending lots of money or if they feel that there is a good connection. Chapter 4 - Men's Wants provides some of the ingredients needed to create good connections with men.

Recommendations: Someone said that you should "Compliment the beauty on their brains and the brainy on their beauty." The gist of this saying is that you don't want to compliment the obvious qualities that someone has. If someone is very wealthy or very successful, try to appreciate the not so obvious qualities that they have. Try to appreciate their hobbies or passions. For example, if they are a musician or they are artistic, show that you appreciate their creative passions. Most people focus on the obvious qualities. Be different - focus on the qualities that are not so obvious.

Number 1 - Childhood

It all begins with childhood. Many of the issues encountered in adult relationships can be traced back to childhood. [15] [16] This is the case because many parents don't sufficiently address their children's emotional needs. [17] As a result, many adults have unresolved issues from childhood. Famous psychoanalysts, such as Sigmund Freud and Erik Erikson, have explored the link between childhood and why people become who they are. [18] How children are raised substantially impacts who they become. [15]

Raising children is very challenging for many parents. It is very difficult for many parents to handle their duties as parents and also think about their children's future relationships. They don't always look 20 years into the future and consider what their children's dating or relationship experiences might be like. As a result, sometimes children's physical needs (food, clothing, shelter, etc.) are met, but their mental and emotional needs are not. When children's mental and emotional needs are not met, they are more likely to experience emotional challenges later in life. [16]

Sometimes emotional challenges are addressed in dating relationships because that is the only time that they are given serious thought. For example, if someone is selfish or distrustful it may not be an issue at their job because their job does not require deep emotional connections with their colleagues. A dating relationship, on the other hand, is much more likely to require a deep emotional connection. If one or both persons in a relationship (including friendship) had unmet needs in childhood, it could make the relationship challenging. This is one of the reasons you may not want someone to be themselves - they have not resolved issues from their childhood.

It's bad enough that children sometimes have unmet emotional needs. To make matters worse sometimes their physical needs are also not met. For example, some children don't have adequate amounts of food or shelter. I had a roommate who told me that he and his family were once homeless, and he recalls having to sleep in a car. Some of his family experiences reminded me of the movie *The Pursuit of Happiness*, featuring Will Smith.

Children need to feel safe. Sigmund Freud said, "*I cannot think of any need in childhood as strong as the need for a father's protection.*" Unfortunately, many fathers are not present to keep their family (including their children) safe. In some cases the fathers are present, but they contribute to a dysfunctional or unhealthy home environment. As a result, children sometimes experience physical abuse or emotional neglect - which can sometimes be traumatic. Here are some common traumatic events that some children experience:

a) **Physical abuse:** Physical punishment, sometimes called corporal punishment, typically involves spankings or beatings. To be clear - I am not saying that spankings or beatings equal child abuse. According to a recent Time magazine article [19] titled "Hitting Your Kids Is Legal in All 50 States", it is legal to use physical punishment or corporal punishment. Unfortunately, there are many studies that show that physical punishment has many negative effects. [16] Physical punishment can lead to aggression, anxiety, depression, post-traumatic stress disorder, and many antisocial behaviors. Physical punishment often does not change a child's behavior it simply delays it into adulthood. [15] Guess who has to deal with the consequences of the physical punishment? You and society.

b) **Emotional neglect:** Children have social and emotional needs that impact their mental health. Mental health is just as important as physical health. Unfortunately children's social and emotional development is not as visible as their physical development. As a result, many busy parents focus on their children's physical needs and pay little or no attention to their emotional needs. I will not elaborate on children's emotional needs because that is a complex subject that can fill a book. I will say however that the second step of the relationship framework - Understand and appreciate the needs and perspectives of others - also applies to children. When children's emotional needs are unmet, it makes it more difficult for them to have healthy adult relationships.

c) **Sexual abuse:** According to The Rape, Abuse & Incest National Network (RAINN), 15% of sexual assault and rape victims are under the age of 12. [20] Sexual assault, in this case, refers to sexual encounters between a child and an adult or encounters between a child and another child. Sexual assault usually involves inappropriate touching, but it can also include behaviors that don't involve touching (such as displaying genitals).

d) **School bullying or violence**: Children sometimes can be cruel. As a result, students sometimes are victims of bullying, fights, violence, and threats of violence. These events can traumatize some students because they don't feel safe as a result.

Recommendations: It is sometimes not easy to discuss issues related to your childhood. You may be unaware that you are affected by childhood issues. This is one of the reasons that mental health professionals recommend regular mental health checkups. Your mental health should be just as important to you as your physical health. In some cultures, there is a stigma associated with mental health therapy. For example, many people don't want to see a psychologist, psychiatrist, or therapist because they don't want to be perceived as "crazy." I suggest to those people that many people are not "crazy" because they invest in their mental health and well-being by seeing a therapist on occasion.

If you think that you have no significant issues, and everyone else has an issue, it's okay. You still need to learn how to interact well with all of those people with issues. Psychologists and therapists understand that you're not the issue. I help those with issues and those without issues all the time.

The List of Things Unsaid

For convenience, here is the list of things unsaid in order of importance.

1. Childhood

2. Money

3. Communication

4. Trauma

5. Sex

6. Love

7. Family

8. Political or world views

9. Health

10. Fears

Chapter Summary

Many of the items in the preceding list are not sufficiently discussed because people are not aware of its importance. For example, you may not be aware of how your childhood or family is affecting your relationships. Or you may not realize that some of your fears are holding you back. It's okay. Everyone has fears and concerns. You can overcome many of your fears and concerns when you discuss them with someone. Step 1 of the relationship framework is to know yourself and invest in yourself so that you can be a better person.

Knowing yourself, in this chapter, means knowing your issues. Everyone has issues, so it's not a bad thing that you have issues. Just make sure that your issues don't control you. Make sure that you are in control.

If you can comfortably talk about an issue, then there is a good chance that you are in control of that issue. Can you have a healthy open discussion about each item on the List of Things Unsaid? If not, find someone who you respect and can trust to discuss your concern or issue. A licensed therapist is probably best. If that is not an option at the moment, then consider talking to a trusted friend or family member. If you are in a dating relationship (or marriage) you should be comfortable discussing each item on the list. Good relationships require good communication.

Step 2 of the relationship framework is to understand and appreciate the needs and perspectives of others. Others' perspectives are sometimes influenced by the issues that they have dealt with or are dealing with at the moment. Step 3 of the relationship framework is to think of the best interaction or relationship that makes sense for you and the other person. It helps to know your issues/challenges and the other person's issues/challenges when determining the best interaction or relationship that makes sense. When you respect and or appreciate someone's issues/challenges you are setting the foundation for a great emotional connection.

Don't Be Yourself: Be a better person

Women's Wants

Men are governed by lines of intellect - women: by curves of emotion.

- James Joyce

Safety, Fun, and Pleasant Surprises

Michelle was the maid of honor for her best friend, Wendy. Wendy loves wine tasting, so Michelle decided to surprise her with a wine tasting bridal shower. She scheduled a trip from Atlanta, Georgia to a popular vineyard in Cleveland, Georgia - one and a half hours away. Michelle, Wendy, some of Wendy's closest friends, and members of the bridal party rode in style in a limousine bus. They listened to several CD's of Wendy's favorite songs from the 80s and 90s while they shared fun stories, told jokes, and took pictures. They arrived at the vineyard a little late, but no one noticed because they had such a great time on the way there. The entire experience was fun and memorable.

Wendy's experience highlights some of the things that women want and appreciate - safety, fun, pleasant surprises, and spending time with thoughtful friends. These things contribute to a sense of security. Men sometimes forget that some of the simple things are important to women. Some men spend money on fancy dinners, pricey events, or costly items as if they hope to buy a woman's affections. Spending a lot of money may work with some women, but many women want deep emotional connections that cannot be purchased. For these women, men's time and resources would be better spent on planning thoughtful, fun, and memorable activities that provide a safe and relaxing environment in which to build trust and create intimacy and connection.

A fun experience can be as simple as a trip to a beach or a park on a nice sunny day. Beaches and parks are often public places - which usually makes them safe during the day. Your experience can include good conversation and pleasant surprises. You and your date can be relaxing and enjoying a lovely day when one or more musicians show up and start playing some pleasant tunes. Or perhaps a magician comes along and entertains both of you. Was it planned or was it a coincidence? Who cares? As long as it is a fun experience.

Night time events can be safe and fun too. A nice dinner followed by a nice walk or dancing at a classy venue can be good ingredients for a fun night. Don't forget to include a pleasant surprise if you can. For example, if you are celebrating a special occasion (birthday, anniversary, celebration, etc.) a special dessert or drink is recommended. In some venues, a musical dedication or shout out from the DJ or band can be a pleasant surprise.

To be clear - if you are successful, and you can afford a limousine ride to a fun place then feel free to add it to your repertoire of things to do. The same goes for a helicopter ride or flight. If you cannot afford (or you're not ready for) the limousine ride or flight, then go someplace local. There are many possibilities. It all depends on you and your date. Think of fun things that you both enjoy.

Note to men: Remember that I said earlier that the more you invest in yourself, the less you have to spend on dates. For example, if you invest in your emotional health and well-being it's much easier to be a positive person. When you invest in your passions, you will have interesting experiences and opinions that can lead to rich conversation. Also, if you invest in your physical health and appearance, you will probably be more confident - which is very attractive. A confident, positive attitude will help you have a fun, successful date.

If you have been paying close attention, you may feel that women want a bit more than safety, fun, and pleasant surprises. You are correct. There is more to it than that. By now you probably realize that I like putting things in lists, so there is a list coming - a list of women's needs and wants. Before we take a look at that list, however, let's look at a few unique things that are unique to women. Two of the most desirable traits that a man can have is the ability to protect his woman and provide for her.

Women Need Protection

A man should keep his woman safe - especially if she is the potential mother (or actual mother) of his child. Keeping a women safe is not limited to being willing to fight to defend her honor. It also includes keeping her emotionally safe. For example, if she is having a difficult time dealing with a mechanic or an insurance agent a man can step in and handle the interaction. If a man's family member (even his mom) does not treat his woman respect, he should (politely) insist that his woman is treated with respect. A man who stands up for his woman helps her feel secure.

Women Want Providers

A man should be able to provide for his woman and his family. He does not have to make the most money to be a good provider. Many husbands make less than their wives, but it is not an issue because they work as a team and make sure everything is taken care of. Even if a man makes less than his wife or significant other, he can still do many of the things expected of a man - fix things (or get them fixed), heavy lifting, provide protection, lead, etc. There are many ways to provide.

One of the reasons men should pay on the first date is that it shows that he can potentially provide. If a man asks a woman out, he should expect to pay. If money is an issue, then the first date can be inexpensive - coffee, ice cream, wine tasting, dessert, pizza, etc. A man can also be creative by planning a picnic in the park, cooking dinner, or thinking of something unique. The key is to make the experience fun. Men should keep in mind that the first date does not have to be dinner.

Most survey results of what women want do not include dinner. The results typically include things like security, good sense of humor, confidence, interesting, reliable, etc. Dates or interactions that exhibit qualities that are important to women tend to be fun dates. If taking a woman to dinner helps you display the important qualities she wants then go ahead and have dinner. Just keep in mind that many women are mindful of their weight/figure. If a woman is slim, she probably wants to stay slim. If she is overweight, she may be reluctant to eat too much. It is sometimes in your best interest to think of something fun that does not involve a lot of food.

The List of Women's Needs and Wants

I have surveyed and interviewed hundreds of women about what they want. I have also looked at other survey results and articles about what women want. There are many lists of men's and women's wants on the Internet. If a list does not include any mention of attraction, looks, or appearance, it is probably not a very accurate list. This list is based on survey results that have been corroborated by other survey results. [21] Without further ado, I present to you the list of women's needs and wants:

The Top 10 Qualities That Women Want in a Man

1. **Safety:** Since ancient times men were expected to keep their women safe. This need is biological and evolutionary. Every woman needs to feel safe - safe with her man and safe from others.

2. **Security:** Women need to feel secure. Commitment, dependability, the ability to provide, and a willingness to listen are some key traits that help a woman will feel

secure. Good eye contact also helps women feel secure. If you have difficulty maintaining eye contact, it might suggest that you are either unfocused or hiding something.

3. **Attraction:** Women need to feel attracted to their men. Attraction is not only about looks. A man does not have to be a pretty boy with nice hair or have a cute baby face. Men can also be considered attractive when they are stylish and well-groomed. Also, men who have many or all of the qualities on this list are very attractive to women.

4. **Love and respect:** Love and respect are very important in relationships. A woman feels loved when she is made the number one priority in her man's life. She feels respected when he listens and appreciates her concerns.

5. **Good morals/character:** Women like men with a good moral compass. For some women, a good moral compass means a relationship with God. For other women, it means spiritual convictions. The key point is for men to have a good sense of right and wrong.

6. **Good communication:** Good communication skills are very important. A woman appreciates when a man can listen to her concerns and can also share his concerns. Men who communicate well help women feel secure.

7. **Confidence:** Confidence is very sexy to women. Confident men are not needy or thirsty. They tend to be relaxed and in control. Think of legendary movie

characters like James Bond or the Godfather - they are always in control.

8. **Sense of humor/fun:** Everyone likes to laugh and have fun - including women. If a man can keep his woman smiling or laughing, he will have a special place in her heart.

9. **Intelligence:** Some intelligence is important because intelligent men are more likely to make intelligent decisions or display good judgment. Women like men who have good judgment - it gives the impression that they can provide.

10. **Ambition/passion:** Women want a man with a plan. Men who are passionate and have goals are very attractive. There is a saying by Benjamin Franklin, "If you fail to plan, you are planning to fail."

Common Traits That Women Want

The List of Women's Needs and Wants is supported by a *Men's Health* magazine survey of over 1,000 American women ages 21 to 54 to find out what traits they want in a man. [21] The traits were placed in one of four categories - character, personality, practical, and physical attributes. The women who completed the survey rated character and personality traits higher than traits related to physical attractiveness. The results are consistent with many studies that show that although looks are important to women, character and personality are more important. Each trait is listed in its category and also in order of importance.

The top 5 character traits

1. **Faithfulness:** Over 80 percent of the women surveyed rated "faithful to me" as an attribute that they find sexy in a man. A man who is faithful is more likely to stick around and support his woman. He lets everyone know that his woman is his. Faithfulness helps women feel secure.

2. **Dependability:** 75 percent of women surveyed said that they want a man who follows through. If a man says that he is going to do something he should do it. Men who follow through are perceived as more likely to commit. They help women feel secure.

3. **Kindness:** This trait is more often appreciated by women who are more mature or women who want a long-term relationship. Younger women are more likely to go for the bad-boy type. Women who want kindness will pay attention to how a man treats people outside of his circle. For example, if a man treats the waiter/waitress nicely he will be perceived as kind.

4. **Moral Integrity:** Honesty is important to men and women. This is especially true when discussing things that can be verified - marital status, children, what you do, etc. Many women feel that men who are honest will be good, caring partners in the long term. One caveat I will add is that the study authors mentioned that white lies are okay. A point that is consistent with my interviews and surveys. I will elaborate more on this in Chapter 9 - Good Communication.

5. **Fatherliness:** Women like men who are good fathers or have the potential to be good fathers. A man who is a good role model is more likely to be a good dad. For example, men who mentor or help young people are perceived as potential good dads. Also, men who are godfathers or spend time with their nieces and nephews are more likely to be good dads. Some of the key qualities that suggest a man will be a good dad are patient, caring, and considerate.

The top 5 personality traits

1. **Sense of Humor:** Laughter has many therapeutic benefits - it helps decrease stress levels, and you burn calories while laughing. If you can enjoy a good laugh or make others laugh, chances are you can handle stressful situations well. Note that you don't have to be a comedian to have a sense of humor. Just make sure that you can appreciate the lighter side of things, and you don't take yourself too seriously. A man who can make a woman laugh gets bonus points.

2. **Intelligence:** Men who are well-rounded usually have interesting experiences or interesting stories to tell. According to the survey results, women like showing off a man who is well-rounded. They also like men who are constantly trying to improve - those men are never boring.

3. **Passion:** According to the survey results, women have a soft spot for musicians because musicians tend to be passionate in public. Many men don't display passion,

or they don't display passion publicly. A man who is comfortable being passionate in public is a breath of fresh air for many women. There are many ways to display passion. You can display passion by speaking in public, painting/drawing, working the grill at a barbecue, singing, doing community service, and more.

4. **Confidence:** I was a little surprised that this did not rank higher in the *Men's Health* survey because it ranked very high in my interviews and surveys. Many women find confidence sexy. Men who are confident are more willing to tackle unfamiliar situations or deal with unfamiliar people. This quality helps women feel secure. I've used the word secure several times. By now you should realize that anything a man does to help a woman feel secure is a great thing.

5. **Generosity:** Women over 35 are more likely to find generosity important according to the survey. Generosity, in this case, is not limited to paying for dates or buying things. It can also refer to a willingness to give time and listen to concerns.

The top 5 practical skills

1. **Listening:** Men who pay attention and listen well help women feel safe and secure. The popular TV sitcom *Frasier* featured a psychiatrist, Frasier Crane, who always said to his radio station callers "I'm listening." The phrase helps put people at ease. Listening is powerful.

2. **Romancing:** Romance appeals to every woman. According to the survey, every woman fantasizes about being swept off her feet. Men who are romantic display a vulnerable side that many women find irresistible.

3. **Being Good in Bed:** Intimacy should start before you are in bed with your partner. A man who takes care of his woman before they are in the bedroom will make the bedroom experiences more pleasurable.

4. **Cooking, cleaning, etc.:** A man who helps with household chores and knows how to make a great meal can win a woman's heart. Studies have shown that cleaning up is foreplay because when a man helps his woman with household chores she will probably feel relaxed. [22] A relaxed woman is a happy woman.

5. **Earning Potential:** Men who are successful in their careers are considered sexy. This is because success often requires ambition, talent, goal achievement, and follow-through. These qualities suggest that a man will be a good provider.

The top 5 physical attributes

1. **Sense of Style:** Remember earlier I discussed *thin slicing* - people make decisions about you based on your appearance. A man's sense of style (or lack thereof) reflects on the woman he is with. A well-dressed man is considered sexy. Also, according to the survey, men who dress well are more likely to notice and appreciate when their woman dresses well. I will add that a sense of style is one of the key ingredients of swag - which we will look

at later. For now, keep in mind that a man should be able to color coordinate, style coordinate, and wear clothes that fit well.

2. **Handsome Face:** Men have a lot of control over some of the key qualities that make them handsome. For example, men who are well groomed (clean cut, nice haircut, neatly groomed facial hair, etc.) are likely to be considered handsome. Also, a man with a nice smile (i.e. nice clean teeth) is more likely to be considered handsome. Every man is different, so it all depends on the man. The point is that every man needs to know (or figure out) which look works best for him and then work towards achieving that look.

3. **Height:** Height is an interesting trait. Some men might think that if they are shorter than 6 feet they are not tall. This is not the case because "tall" is a relative term. A guy can be 5 feet 8 inches and date a woman who is 5 feet 4 inches. In her eyes, he may be considered tall because he is taller than her. Women in the survey reported that they like feeling smaller than their men, but it is not an absolute must. Sometimes shorter men can make women feel loved and secure. If a woman feels loved and secure, she may be willing to change her height preferences.

4. **Muscular Build:** Notice that muscular build is lower on the list. Most women who completed the survey prefer men who are in good overall physical shape without big bulging biceps. Perhaps it's because men who have bulging biceps are very likely to spend a lot of time

maintaining their muscles. For these women, the concern is that the time spent at the gym may limit the quality time spent with her. Also, very big muscular men can be intimidating to some women.

5. **Fitness:** Men who are physically fit give the impression that they are well disciplined or have good self-control. A man who has good self-control is sexy because it suggests that he is confident. Also, women appreciate a man who is physically fit because it suggests that he can keep up in and out of the bedroom.

The Thin Slices

The above list of traits covers character traits and also physical attributes that lead to attraction. Remember the term *thin slicing* - men and women form opinions about you based on your appearance. This is partly because your appearance is in your control. Your clothes, sense of style, posture, hygiene, and physical fitness are all in your control. Very often your appearance and body language say a lot more about you than the words that you say. Sometimes people may get to know you and realize that their opinions about you were incorrect - that is IF they get to know you.

Remember step 1 of the relationship framework - know yourself and invest in yourself so that you can be a better person. Sometimes the easiest investment to make in yourself relates to your outward appearance. If you are a guy having trouble getting dates you should consider one or all of the following:

1. **Upgrade your wardrobe.** Women like a well-dressed man. You don't have to spend money on expensive clothes. You can find name brand clothing at good prices if you search. If there are no good deals in your area, you can use the internet.

2. **Update your grooming habits if necessary.** Women like men who pay attention to details when it comes to grooming. Generally speaking, nice haircuts and neat facial hair will get you points. Some guys can get away with the "untidy" look. If you are unsure about what style looks best on you ask for feedback.

3. **Improve your hygiene related habits.** Men who smell good significantly boost their desirability. Bathe regularly - at least once a day. Also, make sure you have a few bottles of quality cologne and apply a little of it when you are going out. Don't overdo it. People should notice your pleasant scent when they hug you or dance close to you or when you lean in to whisper.

4. **Maintain good body language.** People notice your body language from a distance and form impressions accordingly. This is one of the most common thin slices that people take to determine what you are all about. Bad body language might suggest that you have bad habits. For example, if your head is down or your shoulders droop down some people will think that you lack confidence. Also, if you lean in too much or violate someone's personal space, they may think that you are needy or thirsty. Be sure to read Chapter 7 - The Hungry Don't Get Fed.

Note to Nice Guys

Women sometimes say that they want kind, sensitive, nice, guys, but when given a choice, they reject the kind, sensitive (nice) guys for men with prominent characteristics such as physical attractiveness, swag (see Chapter 5), or intrigue. This typically happens because nice guys are considered boring and predictable. As women get older and want to settle down, they are more likely to date nice guys, but they usually hope that the nice guy has some "bad boy" qualities. The point is that women often don't want guys who are too "nice".

If you are a nice guy, you may sometimes wonder if you are too nice. That depends. If someone is describing you to a friend and the main thing they say is "He's a nice guy" or "He's nice" then it is possible that you are too nice. This is most likely the case if you are having trouble getting dates or getting into a relationship. You should review the list of women's needs and wants and consider making changes. You can keep some of your nice qualities, but you should add other qualities. You want women (and people) to describe you using words like fun, funny, confident, attractive, passionate, interesting, or secure. Women like being able to gush when they talk about their men. The word nice is seldom used when someone is gushing.

Avoid Limiting Beliefs

Sally, a very good friend of mine, made it her mission to travel to every continent (except Antarctica). She also visited many of the popular tourist destinations in the United States such as New York City, Las Vegas, Miami, and places in Hawaii.

Travelling was very important to Sally. As a result, I assumed that Sally and I would not be a good match because she seemed too high maintenance. I could not afford to do the amount of traveling she liked to do.

Sally met a singer named Mike at a singles event. Mike did not have a steady job and, as a result, did not have much money. He also lived at home with his parents. Mike was in his late 20s and did not even have a driver's license. To be fair to Mike, he lived in New York City. Many people in New York City don't have a driver's license because they don't own cars - they rely on the subway and other forms of public transportation. So basically, Mike not having a driver's license is not a terrible flaw - although Sally's mom thought it was a big shortcoming.

Mike made up for his perceived shortcomings because he was one of the most positive people you could meet. He had a great sense of humor, a great voice, and got along really well with people. Sally and Mike began dating and eventually got engaged because Mike was such a great guy. He made Sally feel special. He invested a lot of time in their relationship and always planned fun activities in and around town. What I found fascinating was the fact that Mike and Sally never traveled outside of the U.S. because Mike could not afford it. I don't think they even traveled outside of New York State. After observing their relationship, I made a note to self - do not assume that a woman is a too high maintenance without getting to know her. Avoid limiting beliefs.

Chapter Summary

Step 2 of the relationship framework is to understand and appreciate the needs and perspectives of others (especially the opposite sex). Every woman is different. Some qualities and traits are more important than others. For example, younger women who are not looking for commitment tend to be more interested in fun. Older women, or women looking for commitment, tend to be more interested in security. Men can learn about women's needs and wants by talking to women and paying close attention when they talk about what they like.

The list of women's needs and wants offers core qualities that are important to most women. The list of common traits summarizes the list of women's needs and wants by detailing the top 20 traits that are important to most women. When dating, it is very important to pay attention to details such as your appearance, your likeability, and your overall effect on people. Success is in the details. Please keep in mind that the list of women's needs and wants apply to most (not all) women. There are always exceptions to the rule. Follow step 2 of the relationship framework and learn what is important to the person who you like. Your knowledge can lead to a wonderful relationship.

CHAPTER 4

Men's Wants

To be happy with a man you must understand him a lot and love him a little. To be happy with a woman you must love her a lot and not try to understand her at all.

- Helen Rowland

Understanding Men

Remember the first part of the above quote, *"To be happy with a man you must understand him a lot."* Understanding a man is consistent with step 2 of the relationship framework - understand and appreciate the needs and perspectives of others (especially the opposite sex). To understand a man you should know his needs, wants, and concerns. Chapter 2 talks about topics that are often not discussed or not discussed sufficiently. If you can comfortably discuss many of those topics, you will have a better understanding of the man (or person) in your life.

Men are sometimes not easy to understand because they don't talk about some of the things that are important to them. Some women wonder "What is important to men, besides sex and intimacy?" One way to determine what is important to a man is to look at how he spends his money and his time. Money talks. Time is money, so time talks too. Here is how many men spend significant amounts of time and or money:

1. **Children:** Men who value their responsibilities as fathers (or godfathers) will spend time and money on their kids. If you like children, and you are interested in a man who has children, you will probably get along well.

2. **Pets:** A dog is a man's best friend. Men with dogs spend time and money on their dogs. For example, usually, the dog has to be walked at least twice a day. The dog also has to be fed regularly and taken to the vet periodically. Pets, in general, require time and money. If you can be friendly with a man's pets, you will get points.

3. **Education:** If a man is spending (or borrowing) a lot of money to earn a degree, then his education is very important to him. In this scenario, it would be very helpful to encourage him or commend the fact that he is working on earning his degree. You may be able to establish a good connection if you treat him to lunch (or something similar) when he reaches a milestone like getting a good grade in one of his classes.

4. **Technology** (Computers, TVs, fancy sound systems, music equipment, video games, etc.): Women have comfort food, men have technology. Men enjoy their technology because it helps them relax and unwind. For example, some men enjoy watching TV or movies on a nice large screen TV with a surround sound system. Other men enjoy playing video games with friends (or with strangers on the Internet). The more money a man

spends on technology, the more important it is to him. If you can respect or appreciate a man's technological prowess, you will make a good impression.

5. **Business or special projects:** Some men are ambitious. They want to be successful and are working on becoming successful. For example, a man with a business most likely wants his business to be successful. He may network and attend events that will help his business. Also, a singer or musician who is working on a music album, wants to be famous or successful. As a result, he may perform or participate in events that allow him to promote himself. It helps to encourage a man with a plan.

6. **Cars/vehicles:** Men like status. A luxury (or fancy) car is a status symbol. Remember earlier when we talked about thin slices? A man with a luxury car is perceived as successful. If that luxury car is also a sporty car, it suggests that the driver is fun and successful. You may not know much about cars, but you can still have a conversation about it. For example, you can talk about the color, speed, style, sound system, or anything that is pretty obvious. Luxury car manufacturers put a lot of effort into their cars' features because they want people to talk about it.

The above list does not apply to every man. Every man is different, so it is important to observe and determine how a man likes to spend his time and money. The key point is that men spend money on their passions or favorite items because their passions may provide a sense of accomplishment or fulfillment. For example, after a man gets his degree, he makes himself more marketable and also has a good sense of pride. After a man spends money on technology, he can expect to enjoy that technology.

When a man spends money on dates, it is not clear if he will enjoy the experience. As a result, many men are concerned about spending [what they feel is] too much money too soon. Even financially successful men sometimes don't like spending too much too soon. When I surveyed men, some of them stated that they don't like when women have a sense of entitlement. For example, they don't like when women believe that they should spend a large amount of money on them. Women who understand men's concerns regarding money are ahead of the curve.

Here is another way of looking at it: A confident, mature man knows that when he asks a woman out, he should pay for the date. He also understands that she has every right to not be interested in a romantic relationship after the date. He is, therefore, taking a chance when he asks a woman out because she might not like him romantically, or he might not like her romantically - there might not be a connection. This is all normal and part of the process - it comes with the territory. Usually, the purpose of a date is to provide two people with an opportunity to get to know each other. A great connection is icing on the cake.

Are Men Afraid to Commit?

Women who believe that men are afraid to commit most likely do not understand men very well. These women often

72

ignore or gloss over the fact that there are men who are in committed relationships - husbands, fiancés, and boyfriends. Are those men a rare breed? Were they tricked into committing? The answers are no and no. Clearly some men are not afraid to commit. What about the men who are not in committed relationships? Why have they not committed?

Men who have not committed often have something in common with women who have not committed - they don't want to settle. Think about your smart, attractive, successful, single female friends for a moment. If they are attractive then we can safely assume that there are guys who like them - yet they remain single. Why do they remain single? Most likely it's because they don't want to settle. In some cases, they don't want to settle for a guy who they don't find attractive. In other cases, they don't want to settle for a guy who is not successful, not ambitious, or not on "their level". These are all perfectly valid reasons. The heart wants what it wants - this applies to women and men.

Let's take a look a closer look at what men want. I surveyed 135 men who are over thirty years old, independent, have good jobs, and can support a family if necessary. Most of these men are not in a committed relationship because the women who they have feelings for do not have similar feelings for them. If you think about it, that is the reason most adults are single. If you are single, it is most likely because there are people who you like, but they don't like you the same way. There are also people who like you, but you don't like them the same way.

If a man does not have strong feelings for a woman, or

he is not attracted to her romantically, he is unlikely to commit to her. Also, if a man feels a woman is attractive but he does not feel a special connection he is unlikely to commit to her. Men want inner and outer beauty. They want a woman who has most of the qualities on their list - which may make you wonder "What are the qualities on the uncommitted man's list?" Or more generally, "What do men want?" To answer your question, I present to you the list of men's wants.

The Top 10 Qualities Men Want in a Woman

After surveying and interviewing hundreds of men and reviewing other survey results, I have identified the top 10 qualities that men need or want in a woman.

1. **Understanding:** Remember that, *"To be happy with a man you must understand him a lot and love him a little..."* A Woman should understand what is important to her man. If you are wondering what is important to men the answer is simple - this list.

2. **Sex appeal:** Men want women who they find appealing sexually. A man wants to be able to visualize himself having sex with his woman. For this to happen, he needs to be deeply attracted to her. He needs to feel a physical connection. See Chapter 5 - Sex Appeal - for more details.

3. **Playfulness/fun:** Many men are playful and competitive. If a man plays a sport, he usually will find it refreshing if his woman either plays the sport or appreciates his interest in that sport. She can be on his

team or be his cheerleader. The same applies to non-athletic games or activities such as card games, board games, group games, etc.

4. **Good morals/character:** Women with good morals and character are less likely to be involved in drama. Mature men don't like drama. Also, men think about whether or not a woman would be a good mother for their children. Good morals and good character suggest that a woman will be a good potential mother.

5. **Emotional maturity:** There will be disagreements. Men want women who can disagree without being disagreeable. Emotionally unstable women often blame or criticize their man (or others) for what they are feeling. Men respect women who can share their feelings in an honest, mature manner.

6. **Supportive / encouraging:** Many men have passions and ambitions. Those men want women who are supportive and encouraging. The law of attraction says that positive thoughts lead to positive experiences. A woman who shares her man's positive thoughts will enjoy positive experiences with him.

7. **Good communication:** Men sometimes don't process hints very well. This is because men usually communicate directly with each other and with their friends. For example, if a man wants to go rock climbing he might say "Let's go rock climbing. It will be fun." Or he might say "Do you want to go rock climbing?" If a woman wants to go rock climbing, she might say "I saw

a good deal on a rock climbing trip." Or she might say "Some of my friends are going rock climbing." Typically the man would respond by saying something like "That's nice." Men appreciate women who can say what they want. This also applies to times when a woman has a concern. Men like women who can respectfully share their concerns. Having said that, many men realize that sometimes hinting is inevitable because that's the way it is.

8. **Enjoys sex/intimacy:** Sex and intimacy can be very therapeutic when both people engaging in the act appreciate the experience. Intimacy does not only mean sexual intercourse. Intimacy can include hugging, kissing, cuddling, massaging, etc. Sex, on the other hand, means sexual intercourse and other variations of sexual intercourse. Whether you are intimate or having sex, it should be a fun experience for both parties involved.

9. **Not need/clingy:** Men don't like clingers - women who cling to them as if they have nothing going on in their lives. Confident men appreciate women who have interests, responsibilities, and friends. Time spent apart can be healthy. *Absence makes the heart grow fonder.*

10. **Intelligence:** Women sometimes feel that men want women who make them feel smart. It is more accurate that men want women who don't make them feel dumb. A mature man can date an intelligent woman. He wants a woman with a good head on her shoulders.

How to Appeal to Introverted Men

Remember that in Chapter 1, when discussing the Dating Quiz answers, I said that although introverts are comfortable having conversations with women, they sometimes don't initiate those conversations because they feel that approaching a woman (or anyone) out of the blue would be impolite or an intrusion on their day. Introverts tend to be pretty laid back and take comfort in observing the world around them. They prefer alone time and self-reflecting as opposed to socializing and small talk. Introverts are usually deep thinkers.

According to data from the Myers & Briggs Foundation, over 45% of U.S. men are introverts. Some famous male introverts are Bill Gates, Warren Buffet, Barack Obama, and Mark Zuckerberg. These men are obviously very successful, deep thinkers. There are many benefits to dating an introverted man. Here are a few:

a) **Introverts are often good listeners.** Step 2 of the relationship framework - Understand and appreciate the needs and perspectives of others - is another way of saying listen well. Introverts like to listen because they genuinely want to know more about you.

b) **Introverts appreciate emotional connections.** Introverts value having an emotional connection because it taps into their desire to communicate at a deeper level. The fact that they are better listeners makes it more likely that they will appreciate things that are important to you.

c) **Introverts tend to be laid back.** Introverts generally don't get loud and argumentative. They also don't mind taking a behind the scenes role. If you are an outgoing, people person who loves small talk and socializing, then you might appreciate the balance that an introverted person offers. You can be the life of the party while they can be supportive and in the background.

d) **Introverts are often good with details.** Introverts are more likely to remember special events or important details - which makes sense for someone who listens well. They are also more likely to be organized and punctual.

e) **Introverts tend to be thoughtful and analytical.** Introverts are more likely to think and analyze before speaking or acting. In some scenarios, they may appear to be calculating, but more often than not they are simply thinking of the best or most appropriate response. Thinking and analyzing before you speak or act is a positive quality.

If you wish to appeal to an introverted guy it helps to have conversations that allow you both to communicate well. Here are a few helpful ways to appeal to an introvert:

1. **Choose a quiet (or relatively quiet) environment.** Introverts are less likely to approach women when in loud environments (clubs, parties, concerts, etc.) because loud environments make it difficult to have a good

conversation. Introverts like to listen. It is difficult to listen well if there is a lot of noise in your environment.

2. **Use your social circle to promote you.** If you have friends or family members who know quality, available men let them know that you are looking for a good quality guy, and most likely they will say nice things about you to their introverted friends. They may also say nice things about you to their extroverted friends. The point is for them to say nice things about you. Sometimes a simple reference is all that is needed to get you in the door.

3. **Try online dating.** Introverts like dating profiles because they are filled with details. Even if you don't provide a lot of information on your dating profile, it says a lot about you. Remember introverts like to think and analyze. If you have a well-written profile and some interesting profile pictures, it makes you more intriguing to an introvert. If you don't have a lot of information on your profile, it suggests that you perhaps have not completed your profile, or maybe you are pessimistic about meeting someone online.

The 90-Day Rule: Is it a good idea?

A good friend's mom re-entered the dating scene after her husband passed away. She told me that she was reading a popular book about relationships. I decided to read the book to see what it was all about. I like the author of the book and thought the book was good overall. However, there are some parts of the book that I strongly disagree with. For example, the author suggested that a woman should wait 90 days before having sex. The reason he suggested 90 days is that he had to wait 90 days before getting benefits when he worked for the Ford Motor Company many years ago.

Waiting 90 days is a bad idea. It is silly and risky for several reasons. Before elaborating let me first say that if you want to wait until you are married to have sex that is perfectly reasonable. Research has shown that if you have a healthy balanced dating relationship, waiting until marriage to have sex makes you more likely to have a stable marriage. [23] Unfortunately, many dating relationships are not healthy or balanced.

Note to women: If you are dating a man who has invested a lot of money, time, and emotions in your relationship you really should be clear about why you don't want to have sex. For example, if you are waiting 90 days and you don't explain why you are waiting, it may be a problem. Your man might think that maybe you are having sex with someone else. He might feel that he is being used. Or he might feel that you are a gold digger - someone who uses men for their money. You don't want a guy to think that you are a gold digger (assuming that you are not).

Another potential problem with waiting 90 days is that it highlights the moment when you eventually have sex. Outside of a honeymoon, it is not a good idea to highlight your first time having sex because the experience may not be all that great. Studies have shown that your first sexual experience with someone may not be a smooth one because sex usually improves as you get to know each other better. If a man feels that sex is supposed to be a reward for his 90 days of work he might be more critical of the experience.

So basically, when it comes to sex you have a few options:

1. You can wait 90 days and tell your guy that you are following a timetable set by an author who had to wait 90 days for benefits at a job he had many years ago. You might also mention that the 90-day recommendation is not based on any scientific research, but you are following it because you like the author. This is not the best option.

2. You can resist setting a timetable. You can simply say that you want the time to be right. When you don't set a timetable, a man is more likely to try to get to know you and find out what is important to you. If you take this approach, make sure that your relationship is balanced. After you go on a few dates, don't let him pay for everything - chip in from time to time. Try to invest similar amounts of time and money into your relationship. If you want a healthy relationship, you should try to invest similar amounts of time and money even if you are having sex. You and your mate can discuss the topics in Chapter 2 - Things Unsaid to determine if it is the right time for you.

3. You can set a timetable but don't say what it is. Have a checklist of what is most important to you and

decide if your needs have been met. It is up to you to decide what is important to you and when is the right time for you. If you are unsure about being intimate, then it is probably not the right time for you. You and your mate can discuss the topics in Chapter 2 - Things Unsaid. If you are comfortable discussing the topics in that chapter, then you may have a good foundation for an intimate relationship.

Chapter Summary

Men are not afraid to commit when they are mature, and they meet someone who has some (or most) of the qualities that are important to them. The list of men's needs and wants covers 10 qualities that are important to most men. You can get along very well with a man if you respect his interests and passions. This is assuming that he has healthy interests and passions. The key point is to respect and appreciate things that are important to him.

Some men don't verbally identify some of the things on their list because they feel that it may not be politically correct. For example, some men don't talk about money because they don't want to appear cheap. Some men don't talk about the importance of sex appeal or looks because they don't want to appear too shallow or be politically incorrect. For example, if a man says "I want a woman with sex appeal" some women might think that he is too focused on sex. What those women may not realize is that it is perfectly okay for a man to want a woman with sex appeal. Men are wired to do more for women who they find sexually appealing. I discuss this in more detail in the next chapter - Sex Appeal.

CHAPTER 5

Sex Appeal

I've been out with some extremely beautiful women who have had no sex appeal whatsoever. It really is a lot more than skin deep.

- Rod Stewart

What is Sex Appeal?

Typically, a man wants his woman to be attractive in a sexual way. He wants to be able to imagine himself having sex with her and look forward to the sexual experience. Also, a woman wants to be able to look forward to intimacy with her man. She wants to feel that sex or intimacy with her man will be a pleasant, fulfilling experience. This is true even if they are not having sex at the moment. For example, some couples choose to wait until marriage before having sex. Even in those situations, it is important that the couple looks forward to sex and intimacy with each other because sex is an important part of marriage. Add to that the fact that most men and women want their partner to be faithful to them. It is easier for men and women to be faithful when they feel that their partner is is sexually appealing - which brings us to the question "What is sex appeal?"

A *Psychology Today* article [24] identified four elements of sex appeal: 1) dynamic attractiveness, 2) circumstances, 3) static attractiveness, and 4) self-representation. Before we continue, please understand that everyone has different tastes. One person may think that you have sex appeal while another person may feel different. The great thing about sex appeal is that it is very much in your control. Let's take a closer look at the four elements of sex appeal.

The Four Elements of Sex Appeal

1) **Dynamic attractiveness:** Some people are not born with great natural looks. They may not have a baby face or an exotic look, but they have dynamic attractiveness. This is because they express themselves in a very intriguing, fascinating, or captivating way. For example, musicians, entertainers, dancers, and actors/actresses sometimes have captivating body language that their fans find appealing. Charisma can also make someone dynamically attractive. Some comedians, motivational speakers, and leaders have a charismatic personality that is very attractive. Body language, confidence, and passion are key ingredients of dynamic attractiveness. If you have fun, easy-going, positive vibe, many people will find you attractive.

2) **Circumstances:** Your situation matters. If you and your partner (or date) are both in a great mood, then you both become more appealing to each other. If both of you enjoy doing things together, you both become more attractive to each other. Research has shown that if you do something fun or exciting with someone, you may

attribute some of those fun feelings to the person you are with and become more attracted to them.

3) **Static attractiveness:** Static attractiveness refers to features that you are born with and also includes features that don't change easily. For example, the shape of your face, your eyes, your nose, and your lips don't change unless you have plastic surgery. Your body shape does not change easily, but you can control your body shape by dieting and exercising. Men often pay more attention to physical features than women do. For example, some men prefer a woman who is in good physical shape. Sometimes it's because they fantasize about being able to pick up her up and spin her around.

4) **Self-representation:** Self-representation refers to how you present yourself - your general appearance. You can make yourself more physically attractive by grooming yourself regularly, using appropriate amounts of makeup, maintaining a current hairstyle, and having a good sense of style. The clothes that you wear should be current, trendy and appropriate for your body type. Avoid wearing anything too big or too small. Another key part of your self-representation is how you smell. Pleasant smells have pleasant effects - especially during intimacy. Make sure your private areas and erogenous zones have a pleasant or neutral smell.

Notice that most of the elements of sex appeal are well within your control. You determine your level of sex appeal. Whether you are a man or a woman, if you are a genuinely fun person, and you take care of yourself then you probably have sex appeal. You will benefit from having sex appeal even if you are not having sex. You will also benefit from having sex appeal even if you are not dating or are not in a relationship. Your sex appeal contributes to your attractiveness. People are generally nicer to people who they find attractive.

Men tend to spend more time/money on women who they feel have sex appeal. Men also spend more time/money on things that they feel have sex appeal. For example, if a man likes his car there is a good chance that he will spend more time/money than necessary on that car. He will spend money to keep it clean and in good condition. He will take it to the shop more often to make sure all is well. He may even add unnecessary things like fancy rims, an enhanced sound system, tinted windows, or any number of features that you can imagine from the movie *The Fast and The Furious*. The bond between a man and what he likes can be very strong.

Sense and Sex Appeal

Remember that in Chapter 2 - Things Unsaid - we looked at some of the requirements for a physical connection. A good physical connection exists when you and your partner (or person of interest) like each other's physical qualities and appearance. To create a good physical connection you should appeal to your partner's five senses - sight, hearing, taste, smell, and touch. Let's take a closer look at how to appeal to the five senses:

1. **Sight** - Men and women have visual desires. Some women like a well-dressed man and some men

appreciate a classy looking woman. Some women want a man with an edgy look, and some men want a woman with a nice body who wears tight, revealing outfits. Some women want a combination - a man who can be well-dressed on some days and edgy on other days. Some men also want a combination - a woman who can look classy on some days and tantalizing on other days. Men and women want to like what they see - which is why your appearance is important.

2. **Hearing** - Everyone appreciates a positive, sociable person. For example, men and women appreciate a good sense of humor. One of the obvious ways to display a good sense of humor is to say funny or amusing things. Funny or amusing things satisfy people's auditory desires. You can also satisfy someone's auditory desires if you are a good conversationalist, a singer, a poet, a rapper, or a motivational speaker. If your voice (or the things that you say) entertains those around you then you then you satisfy their auditory desires.

3. **Taste** - No they don't have to taste you. Sure you can put food or tasty cremes on your body, but you're probably not at that point yet. The suggestions here are generalized so that you can apply them in a variety of scenarios. A simple way to appeal to someone's sense of taste is to introduce them to new cuisines. New cuisines can be fancy meals or simple deals. The goal is to introduce new tastes.

4. **Smell** - There are many lotions, creams, and pleasant fragrances that can appeal to the olfactory senses and

boost your sex appeal. You don't have to wear expensive perfume or cologne. Just make sure you smell good. Also, make sure that you have good hygiene habits and a tidy environment. Many romantic moments are curtailed because of unpleasant odors. Invest in pleasant fragrances for you and your environment.

5. **Touch** - A pleasant touch can be very therapeutic. Sometimes your partner wants to touch you because you take care of your skin. Perhaps you are fortunate to have naturally nice skin. Or perhaps you use a good combination of soaps and lotions and as a result, you have nice skin. There are also times when your partner wants you to touch them because they like your hands. Men and women have tactile desires which can be satisfied with a pleasant touch.

What is Swag?

Swag comes from the word swagger - which means to walk or strut in a bold, defiant manner. Swag typically is used to describe men who are confident and have a unique style. Men who have swag don't worry about what other people think about their style. A man with swag might wear something unique that raises some eyebrows, but he wears it with such confidence it is not an issue. For example, he might wear long pointy shoes with intricate designs that are unfamiliar to most. He wears what he wants and wears it well. A man with swag is cool and relaxed. He is not easily rattled. He has a sense of pride, but he is not boastful or arrogant. Many women love men with swag.

One of the key things about swag is that people with swag were not born with swag. They basically adopted certain mannerisms - usually over a period of time - and kept those mannerisms because they liked the results. For example, when you are confident and you have a sense of style, men and women are more likely to treat you with respect. As a result, you may be motivated to continue having confidence and a sense of style.

There are many ways to develop or boost your confidence. A simple search phrase like "how to boost your confidence" will yield many results. Here are some simple ways to boost your confidence:

Seven Ways to Boost Your Confidence

1. **Maintain good body language:** Pay close attention to the body language of world leaders and prominent leaders in general. Their posture is often polished. When you have good body language, you project confidence. Imagine yourself as a very successful person who is about to make big things happen. People are watching you. They are looking for confirmation that you can make big things happen. Don't let your body language disappoint them.

2. **Update your wardrobe if necessary:** Pay attention to details when you dress. Avoid wearing baggy or oversized clothes. Suits and clothes should be tailored for your physique. Also, make a note of what works well for you with regards to style and colors. Solicit feedback from people with good fashion sense. For example,

people who work at clothing stores typically have a lot of fashion sense.

3. **Be positive:** Avoid the wet blankets and Debbie Downers. Surround yourself with positive people. Speak positively of others when you can. When you speak positively about someone, it makes you seem positive. Also, sharing positive stories or experiences make you seem positive.

4. **Maintain good eye contact:** Looking someone in the eye usually happens naturally when you are comfortable or confident. If you have difficulty making eye contact with others you can practice in low-risk settings. For example, when you are ordering food you can make eye contact while speaking to your waiter/waitress. When you are out shopping, you can make eye contact with the person helping you. You should look people in the eye about 60 to 70 percent of the time when speaking to them.

5. **Listen more, talk less:** It is very helpful to understand and appreciate the needs and perspectives of others. For this to happen, you need to listen well. The more you listen, the more you learn.

6. **Speak clearly:** If people often ask you to repeat yourself, it is possible that you are not speaking clearly. It is also possible that you are speaking to fast. Slow down your speech and you'll notice a difference.

7. **Be polite and respectful:** Confident people don't say mean things or criticize others. A confident person is secure and does not feel a need to lower the value of others. If a critical opinion is necessary, a confident

person can be critical without being cruel. The key point is to be polite and respectful.

Chapter Summary

Many men and women want you to do your best and be your best. For example, a man might not have a baby face and nice hair but if he grooms himself well, has good body language, and is confident then he has sex appeal. A woman might not have an exotic look and long natural hair, but if she has a great fun attitude, dresses well, and takes care of her body, she has sex appeal. The key theme of the four elements of sex appeal is that you can and should do your best with what you have.

Step 1 of the relationship framework is to know yourself and invest in yourself so that you can be a better person. Your sex appeal is in your control. You can invest in yourself by engaging in activities that contribute to your dynamic attractiveness, your static attractiveness, and your self-representation. Step 2 of the relationship framework is to understand and appreciate the needs and perspectives of others (especially the opposite sex). Men and women love sex appeal. They want their partner to be appealing sexually. Your sex appeal will set the foundation for a good physical connection.

CHAPTER 6

Why Men Don't Approach

Thinking will not overcome fear but action will.

- W. Clement Stone

Why Men Don't Approach

Many smart, attractive, single women sometimes wonder why men don't approach them. Some of these women think that men are too shy or too scared to approach them. I've always had a pretty good idea as to why men don't approach, but I decided to do a survey to be sure. I surveyed 150 men to find out why they don't approach women who they find attractive. Here are some of the most common reasons single (and available) men don't approach women who they find attractive:

1. **Fear of rejection:** Some men are afraid to approach a woman because they worry that the woman will turn them down or not be interested in them. This condition is sometimes referred to as *approach anxiety*. I will discuss how to overcome approach anxiety in Chapter 8. Keep in mind the fact that many men fear rejection because they have been rejected so don't be too hard on them.

2. **They are not thinking about approaching:** Men are sometimes focused on things other than women. For

example, if a man is shopping for a new TV or computer he may not notice the very attractive woman that walked past him. Also, some men don't dress their best when not on a date or when not looking for a date. As a result, they may not feel their best at the moment. If a man does not feel his best, he is less likely to approach.

3. **Some men are introverts:** According to data from the Myers & Briggs Foundation, over 45% of U.S. men are introverts. An introvert may think that a woman is attractive and also be comfortable not approaching her. An extrovert is more likely to be uncomfortable with the fact that he did not approach. For example, some guys regret not approaching a woman they felt was attractive or interesting.

> **Quick note:** Do not to confuse introversion with fear of talking to women. There is a character on the TV sitcom *The Big Bang Theory*, who is terrified of speaking to women unless he is drunk. This condition is known as selective mutism. Introverts are not afraid of speaking to women. They are simply comfortable not initiating conversations.

4. **They are dating someone or in a relationship:** Many men feel that one woman is enough. If they are in a relationship, they are less likely to approach another woman with dating in mind. Also, if a man is getting to know someone and he feels that there is good potential for a happy relationship he is also less likely to approach a woman with dating in mind.

5. **They don't have to:** Some men look good and as a result, they are used to being approached. They may be wondering why you are not approaching them.

A common factor in the reasons for not approaching is that the men are being themselves. Men who are afraid of rejection are playing it safe by not approaching. This is one of the problems with being yourself – you sometimes play it safe and miss out on a potentially good experience. One of the best ways to overcome your fear is to confront it. To paraphrase Franklin D. Roosevelt, "You have nothing to fear but fear itself." I discuss how to overcome approach anxiety in Chapter 8.

Should women approach men?

Women sometimes wonder if it is okay to approach a man. The answer is yes. Here are some of the most common reasons women don't approach men who they find attractive:

1. **They feel that the man should approach:** Many women feel that even in this day and age, with feminism and women's rights, the man should approach. Women often feel that men who approach them are more confident than men who don't.

2. **Fear of rejection:** No one likes to be rejected – including women. Women typically invest a lot more in their appearance than men do. For example, women generally spend more time (and money) on their hair, makeup, outfit, shoes, etc. Imagine doing all of that and then getting turned down.

3. **They don't know how:** Some women seldom have to approach because they get approached often. Other women don't approach because of the reasons listed above. As a result, they don't know how to approach.

If you feel that men should approach you are correct. Men should take the initiative and approach women who they find attractive. The problem is that sometimes a man is not thinking about approaching because he is focused on something else. This can be a good thing because most women don't want a man who will approach every attractive woman he sees. That man might be a player. If a man is focused on a task and does not approach, that might mean that he focuses pretty well. Also, let's face it, women multitask better than men so it should not be surprising that a man might be mission-driven and not pay attention to the pretty women around him. In those situations, women can approach by making casual conversation.

If you are a woman who does not approach because you are afraid of rejection, then you should try to overcome your fear of rejection. Once again, you have nothing to fear but fear itself. The information in Chapters 4 and 5 will help you. Men like confident women who are comfortable initiating conversation. Think of your approach as you initiating casual conversation. Don't expect too much from it because it is just a casual chat. If it leads to a date or a relationship, then that is a bonus - icing on the cake. If it leads instead to a networking opportunity or friendship, then that is also a positive outcome.

Chapter Summary

Approaching the opposite sex is not easy. Men and

women have various reasons for not approaching. Sometimes their reasons are based on their experiences. All reasons for not approaching are valid and should not be belittled. Sometimes men don't approach because they are afraid of rejection. Men should take steps to overcoming their fear of rejection. I provide specific recommendations in Chapter 8 - How to Overcome Approach Anxiety.

Women should consider approaching men on some occasions because men are sometimes preoccupied and not thinking about approaching women. For some women, a focused man may be a great catch. If you are a woman who is nervous about approaching men, don't think of it as an approach. Simply start a casual conversation with no expectations. Sometimes you get more when you expect less.

CHAPTER 7

The Hungry Don't Get Fed

Patience is not simply the ability to wait - it's how we behave while we're waiting. - Joyce Meyer

You Can Get What You Don't Need

In some countries, such as the United States, when you don't need a loan it is easy to get a loan. For example, if you have good credit, you may occasionally receive checks in the mail from lenders. The checks are basically loans that you did not apply for. All you have to do is deposit the check to agree to the terms of the loan and activate it. Lenders are often eager to give you a loan when they know that you don't need the loan. You are more appealing to them when you don't need them. This is often the case in the dating world. People are sometimes more interested in you when you don't seem interested in them.

I am not suggesting that you play games or pretend not to be interested in someone when you actually are interested in them. I am suggesting that you should have hobbies, interests, passions, or activities that occupy your time and make you more appealing. Healthy interests and activities can help you improve as a person and also prevent you from being too needy. For example, if you take gym classes or play a sport, you are helping your body and keeping busy.

Many people will appreciate the fact that you have an active lifestyle and that you have things going on in your life other than dating. Remember that in the introduction I said: "When you interact with someone for the first time, or you are in the early stages of dating, you do not want to appear too eager, needy, or hungry for affection – some refer to this behavior as being thirsty." Your active lifestyle and interests will give potential dating prospects the impression that you are not too anxious or eager to get into a relationship. In other words, potential dating prospects will not think that you are thirsty.

Are You Thirsty?

Thirstiness is all about balance. In a balanced relationship, both people invest similar amounts of time or effort in the relationship. If you are romantically interested in someone, and they do not have a similar level of interest, you might come across as thirsty if you pursue them too much. It is okay to periodically remind someone that you are interested in them, but it should be done in a non-needy charming way. For example, an occasional call or message can communicate that you were thinking about them and that you are not obsessed with them. People often feel uncomfortable if they feel that you are obsessed with them.

If you call or text someone a lot, and they don't respond, then you should take a step back because you might be coming across as thirsty. If someone does not return your call or text after a day or two, they are most likely not interested in you. You can call or text them again to be sure. Just keep in mind that if you call or text them two or three times, and they don't respond, they are most likely not into you. There are a few exceptions to this rule. For example, if someone is traveling out of the country they might not receive your messages while traveling. Also, if someone is hospitalized, they might not receive your message. Use your instincts or talk to trusted friends to see if you are coming on too strong. Men and women sometimes need time to warm up to someone they don't know, or don't know very well. Women typically need more time than average to warm up to men they don't know. Therefore, men should make an extra effort not to appear needy or anxious when pursuing a woman.

Pursue With Patience

Anxious, needy men often make women feel uncomfortable. Confident men, on the other hand, make women feel comfortable. Women want to feel that a man will not flip out or lose it because they are not interested in him. A confident man is not bothered or flustered when a woman does not reciprocate his interest in her. He respects her right to take her time in matters of love or dating. He allows her to follow her heart. A confident man also knows that if a woman is not interested in him, and he handles her disinterest with calm and dignity, she might change her mind in the near future. Many married women readily admit that they did not like their husbands when they first met, but they changed their mind after time passed and they got to know him better.

Men also sometimes change their minds. Sometimes a man may not want to start a serious relationship with a woman because he is simply not ready or he feels that it is too soon. Here are some common reasons that men don't want to get serious but may change their mind later:

a) **They are not ready.** Men sometimes have a to-do list that needs to shrink before they enter into a serious relationship. After they do most or all of what is on their to-do list, they may be ready to get serious. In this type of scenario be supportive if you can. If a man says that he is not ready, it is possible that he is not into you. It is also possible that he really is not ready.

b) **They need more information.** Some women (and men) are reserved, and that is fine, but when a woman is reserved the man knows less about her. When a man is ready to get serious, he will want to feel a good connection with the woman he is interested in. If he feels that she is too reserved, he may feel that there is not a good connection. Women (and men) can share their ideas or interests without revealing too much about themselves. For example, you can talk about your favorite foods, music, passions, celebrities, and more to help you not appear too reserved.

c) **Their potential partner does not have sex appeal at the moment.** In chapter five I mentioned that your sex appeal is in your control. You can probably think of some celebrities (male and female) who had no sex appeal when they were younger, but they cleaned up nicely. Also, many celebrities (and non-celebrities) look very plain, and sometimes unappealing, when they don't have on makeup or nice clothes. When they put on the nice clothes, do their hair, and apply the right amount of makeup they have sex appeal. This doesn't mean that women need to revamp their entire appearance. Sometimes a man simply needs to know that his woman can have sex appeal.

d) **They are sowing their wild oats.** Men and women sometimes go through a phase of simply wanting fun and or sex. During that phase serious or long term relationships seem boring. Most men will eventually grow out of the "sowing wild oats" phase and decide that it's time to settle down.

Patience is a virtue - especially when you like someone romantically. If you pursue someone in an anxious or obsessed manner, you may give the impression that you are trying to control them or force them to be interested in you. For example, if you constantly suggest and the other person never suggests any activities, there is a good chance that they are not interested in you at the moment. In such scenarios, it is best to take a step back and focus on something else. Remember the ballad by blues singer/songwriter Bonnie Rait: *"Cause I can't make you love me if you don't. You can't make your heart feel something it won't."* Men and women like to have autonomy. They value their freedom and independence, especially in dating and relationships. If they are not interested in you don't be anxious, be patient. Keep in mind that you are not interested in everyone who likes you so try to empathize.

It can be disappointing and or frustrating when someone is not interested in you. You can do great things with your frustration. Frustrated energy can be used in a very constructive way. You can convert your frustrated energy to positive energy and do things that can greatly benefit you. Here are some ideas:

a) **Take an improvisation or acting class.** There are many classes that you can take to learn acting or improvisation. You can also take comedy classes. You don't have to be born a comedian; you can learn to be funny.

b) **Watch funny videos or movies.** Laughter is good medicine. Thanks to sites like YouTube you can find many funny video clips - short clips and full comedy routines. You can listen to your favorite comedian or listen to a comedian who you never heard before.

c) **Learn to play an instrument or DJ.** Thanks to software and technology, learning to DJ is easier than ever. Who knows, you could become the next DJ Jazzy Jeff or the next David Guetta. The great thing about DJing is that even if you don't become famous, you can have lots of fun.

d) **Paint or draw.** Painting on canvas or painting a room can be very relaxing. Many home improvement stores, such as Home Depot or Lowes, offer free classes to help you learn the basics.

e) **Meditate or take yoga classes.** Yoga and or meditation classes should be required in school because the potential benefits are tremendous. For example, yoga and meditation can help decrease stress. [25]

f) **Learn a new language.** You can learn to speak a new language with software such as the Rosetta Stone® or you can learn some basics with apps such as Google Translate.

g) **Develop a new hobby.** There are many new hobbies and activities that you have yet to learn. The possibilities are endless.

h) **Find someone who actually likes you, and who you like, and pursue them**. When someone truly recognizes your potential and what you have to offer, and you do the same for them, true love can blossom.

When you use your time and energy to learn new things you become more interesting and perhaps fascinating. In other words, you become a better person. Fascinating people were not born fascinating. They simply learned fascinating things. They have passions and experiences that they either share or demonstrate. For example, if you learned (or know) a second language you can sprinkle your conversations with words or phrases from your second language - which most people will find amusing. Also, if you heard a funny joke, you can share that joke. Even if others don't find it funny, they will appreciate the fact that you find it funny or that you enjoy telling it because a positive a vibe can be very contagious. People enjoy being around people who are having a good time.

The Thirsty Test

Let's test your thirst with a short five question multiple choice quiz. These questions apply to dating and relationship scenarios involving adults. There are no wrong answers. There are simply good answers and better answers. Select only **one answer** for each question. You will get points for each question answered.

1) **If a man gets a woman's phone number, when should he call her?**

    A. It depends on the vibe

    B. Two or three days later

    C. The next day

2) **How many active online dating site accounts do you have?** *Active, in this case, means that you login a few times a week or more.*

    A. Less than 3 (includes none)

    B. Only 3 to 5

    C. More than 5

3) **Do you send friend requests to people on Facebook because you think they're hot?**

    A. No or not really.

    B. Yes. Every now and then.

    C. Yes. That is the main reason I use Facebook.

4) **How often do you think about sex?**

    A. Once a day or less.

    B. A few times a day.

    C. All the time - including now.

5) **Do you dress for attention (you want people of the opposite sex to notice you)?**

    A. No or not that often.

    B. Yes, usually when socializing or going on a date.

    C. Yes. All the time.

Thanks for taking the quiz. We will go over your results after the next section.

Honesty and Thirst

Men and women sometimes say that they want a partner who is honest – this is sometimes inaccurate and misleading. For example, if you are ready to settle down and start a family and you mention that on a first date, you are being honest. If the other person has a romantic interest in you, then they won't mind you sharing the fact that you are ready to settle down. If on the other hand, the other person is not ready to settle down with you, they may feel that you are needy or thirsty. Thirstiness has a lot to do with timing.

Guys sometimes wonder what to say to women because they don't want to say the wrong thing. For example, if a guy sees a woman wearing an outfit that highlights her curves, and he feels that she has nice curves, he may decide to approach her and tell her that she has nice curves. If the woman is not attracted to him, she may feel uncomfortable with his compliment. If his delivery is bad, she might feel that he is creepy. Men also sometimes feel uncomfortable with compliments. For example, if a woman compliments a guy's physique and he is not attracted to her he might feel uncomfortable.

Whether or not you are perceived as needy or creepy

usually depends on you, your timing, and your delivery. If you are confident and a bit detached when you compliment someone it is much less likely that you will be perceived as needy or creepy. Compliments are sometimes best if they seem like a casual observation. You can give direct compliments if the person you are interacting with seems friendly and happy to be with you.

Note to men: Pay close attention to how women interact with you. Women usually avoid touching men who they don't like. The touch rule states that if a woman is touching you, she probably has some level of romantic interest. Note that this rule does not apply to working girls (i.e. prostitutes) or strippers - they want money from you so they will be friendly and probably touch you. This rule also does not apply to women who want you to spend money on them (buying drinks, buying gifts, etc.). The touch rule refers to women in social settings who are being genuinely friendly without immediate expectations.

Thirsty Test Answers

Let's review your Thirsty Test answers. For this test the lower your score, the less thirsty you are. If you chose A as the answer, you get 0 points for that question. If you chose B, you get 1 point for that specific question. If you chose C, you get 2 points for that question. You can get a maximum of 2 points for each question. Your total score should be between zero and 10. Here is an explanation of the best answers:

Question 1: If a man gets a woman's phone number, when should he call her? **Best Answer:** *It depends on the vibe.*

It depends on the vibe created during the interaction. For example, if the conversation went well and the woman either offered her phone number or was happy (smiling or in a good mood) when giving her phone number it is okay for a man to call the next day. Also, if a woman says something along the lines of "You can reach me after ____ time." Or she says "Make sure you call me" it is okay for a man to call the next day. It also helps if the initial conversation lasted for longer than 20 or 30 minutes. If you have a long, interesting conversation with someone, it makes sense to talk the next day because you can continue conversing and getting to know each other.

If, on the other hand, the conversation was brief or it seems as if there was not a strong connection it is okay for a man to call two or three days later. You can also send a text shortly after you get someone's number and say something along the lines of "Hi. This is _____. It was nice meeting you." You can then gauge the response to that text to determine how to proceed. Texting also works for women who exchange numbers with a man and want to say hello without appearing thirsty. A polite text indicating that it was nice meeting or interacting is a nice touch.

Question 2: How many active online dating site accounts do you have? **Best Answer:** *Less than 3*

Less is best in this case. If you follow the guidelines and suggestions in the previous chapters, you should not need an active profile on too many dating sites.

Question 3: Do you send friend requests to people on Facebook because you think they're hot? **Best Answer:** *No or not really.*

Sending friend requests to people who you don't know is not a good look. Invest in yourself and attend social events. If you prefer to stay online, use a dating site to meet people.

Question 4: How often do you think about sex? **Best Answer:** *Once a day or less.*

Once again less is best in this case. If you find yourself thinking about sex a lot, you might want to consider engaging in fun, healthy activities that take your mind off of sex. Find a hobby or do something that you are passionate about.

Question 5: Do you dress for attention? **Best Answer:** *No or not that often.*

It's very important to pay attention to how you dress and your overall appearance. People notice many details that you may not be aware of. The key thing is not to overdo it. People who want to connect with you will pay more attention to your overall personality and body language. People who are simply interested in your body will pay more attention to how you are dressed. It all depends on what or who you want.

Thirsty Test Scores

Your total score should be between 0 and 10 points. If your total score is not between 0 and 10 points, please re-calculate your total score. Remember that if you chose A as the answer, you get 0 points for that question. If you chose B, you get 1 point for that specific question. If you chose C, you get 2 points for that question. You can get a maximum of 2 points for each question. Here is the score breakdown:

i. **0 to 3 points:** Your score is impressive. You are not thirsty - you are well hydrated. You are probably a disciplined and focused person. Continue investing in yourself. There are many opportunities ahead of you.

ii. **4 to 7 points:** Your score is average. You have an average amount of thirst. Make sure that you review (and maybe highlight) some of the key points made in this Chapter. Also, make sure you read Chapter 5 - Sex Appeal.

iii. **8 to 10 points:** You have a high amount of thirst. Try to find activities that relax or intrigue you. For example, consider activities such as yoga, meditation, art, board games, sports, or fishing. The more relaxed or active you are, the less thirsty you will be.

Chapter Summary

Many men and women want to feel that you have a life apart from them. Your hobbies and interests contribute to a sense of balance in your relationships (friendships, dating, and marriage). This sense of balance is very important in the early stages of a relationship because it sets the tone. If you seem anxious and needy in the beginning, people will think that you are an anxious, needy person. If you have interests and hobbies, in the beginning, people will think that you are an interesting person.

The Thirsty Test is a fun way to measure your level of thirst. If you scored high on the test, make some adjustments so that you don't give off thirsty vibes. Find fun things to do that shift your focus away from dating and finding someone. If you scored low on the Thirsty Test, keep up the good work. You are on a great path.

CHAPTER 8

How to Overcome Approach Anxiety

The way to develop self-confidence is to do the thing you fear and get a record of successful experiences behind you.

- William Jennings Bryan

Don't Fear Mistakes

In western countries school often teaches students to avoid making mistakes. For example, when you take a test or write a paper you usually lose points when you make mistakes. If you make too many mistakes, you get a failing grade. Your fear of failure can cause you to fear making a mistake. As a result, you may play it safe and not take risks. Playing it safe sometimes results in missed opportunities. For example, when you don't approach someone who interests you, you are missing an opportunity to learn. Whenever you initiate a conversation, you are learning from that conversation and also improving your conversation skills - which should be your primary goal.

Sometimes you don't initiate conversations with people who you don't know because you are afraid of saying the wrong thing. Or perhaps you are afraid that you will have nothing in common and the conversation will be pointless. Conversations are never pointless. Even if you learned that you have nothing in common with someone you still learned something. Conversations also help you sharpen your instincts because you are more likely to read people accurately when you are comfortable talking to them and listening to them. This can help improve your confidence and also help you build better relationships.

The Conversation Framework

Remember earlier (in the Introduction) I mentioned the Relationship Framework. The steps in the relationship framework are 1) know yourself and invest in yourself so that you can be a better person, 2) understand and appreciate the needs and perspectives of others (especially the opposite sex), and 3) think of the best interaction or relationship that makes sense for you and the other person. This framework can be applied to conversations. Think of a conversation as a brief relationship (a mini-relationship) with 3 phases:

1) **Say a little about yourself.** There are many ways to start a conversation. One way is to start with a general or funny observation about something you like or something that you noticed. Don't start with compliments about how the person looks - it might make them uncomfortable. Keep your very first statement simple or funny. Then pay attention to the other person's reaction. If they seem receptive or open to conversing with you, then go ahead and introduce yourself. You should introduce yourself because people are more comfortable with you when they know more

about you. It sets them at ease and makes them more willing to share information about themselves.

2) **Ask questions that help you learn about them.** It's best to ask simple questions when you first get to know someone. For example, instead of asking "Where do you work?" or "What do you do?" it is better to ask "What do you enjoy doing?" or "Who's your favorite comedian?" Your goal should be to try to identify things that they enjoy talking about. Some people like talking about themselves. Some people like talking about their passions and hobbies. Everyone is different, so you have to pay attention to what makes the other person light up and talk.

3) **Decide what is the best interaction to have going forward.** Based on the conversation, and your observations, you can decide how to proceed. Should you keep in touch? Should you get their number to ask them out on a date later? Or should you simply be friends? It's up to you. It all depends on how you feel about the interaction.

I know that even with the suggestion of a conversation framework some people still struggle to approach people who they don't know - especially people of the opposite sex. I don't want you to miss out on opportunities because you are afraid to approach. For the rest of this chapter, I will not mention approaching or suggest that you approach someone who you don't know. I will simply suggest that you be friendly and initiate conversations.

Seven Things That You Can Do to Improve Your Conversation Skills

1. **Socialize more often:** One of the most commonly suggested ways to meet people is to "go out and socialize." Sometimes you do not socialize well because you are on your phone. If you are constantly on your phone (texting, playing games, reading social media posts, etc.), you are probably missing out on a few opportunities. Put down your phone and embrace your environment. Pay attention to what is happening around you. You might notice someone smiling at you.

2. **Immunize yourself:** Immunization is the process of making you immune or resistant to an infectious disease. Usually, it involves injecting you with a vaccine that contains a small or weakened form of the disease germ. The weakened form of the disease causes your body to create antibodies to fight the disease. As a result, when your body encounters the actual disease it remembers it and also remembers how to fight it effectively it. Your mind and body are remarkably capable of remembering challenging experiences and building a resistance to those challenges. This can help you interact more confidently with people because you will learn that you can overcome any challenging experiences that you have during a conversation. For example, if you initiate a conversation, and it does not go well most likely it's not a big deal. This is especially true if you follow the recommendations from previous chapters and invest in yourself. People usually respond

positively when you initiate casual conversation. If they don't respond positively, it might be because they are dealing with some issue that has nothing to do with you. With practice, you learn to deal effectively with the challenges you face during conversations.

3. **Practice, practice, practice:** Practice makes perfect. This is true when building your conversation skills. Think of how easy it is for you to ride a bike, drive a car (or another type of vehicle), or play your favorite game/sport. When you first started, you made mistakes but now, after years of practice, you're a pro. The same can happen when you have conversations. Don't think about approaching. Simply think about starting light, casual conversations and learning from those conversations. You can have casual conversations while waiting in line at a store, waiting for a class/program to start, or playing a sport. There are many more examples. The point is to make use of your down time and get to know those around you.

4. **Take small risks:** Don't be afraid to take small risks. For example, starting a conversation with someone who you find interesting is a small risk. A popular quote explains it well *"Fear stifles our thinking and actions. It creates indecisiveness that results in stagnation. I have known talented people who procrastinate indefinitely rather than risk failure. Lost opportunities cause erosion of confidence, and the downward spiral begins"* - Charles Stanley. Share pleasant experiences or funny stories. If you have conversations

while you are in a good mood, you will improve your conversation skills.

5. **Wear interesting clothes or items:** A simple way to start a conversation is to wear a conversation piece or invest in a conversation piece. A conversation piece can be a unique thing that you are wearing or a unique thing that you are carrying. For example, sometimes you buy things when traveling that may be unique in your hometown. If someone compliments you or asks about your conversation piece, you can thank them and tell them where you purchased it. Conversation pieces can lead to casual conversations that flow naturally.

6. **Speak positively about others:** Think about people who you respect and admire. If you keep a journal, it is helpful to make an entry about those people and why you respect and admire them. More importantly, make sure that you are comfortable talking about people who you respect and admire. There is a psychological term known as *spontaneous trait transference.* In a nutshell, this term refers to the fact that when you talk about other people, the good or bad qualities you describe are associated with you. For example, if you speak negatively about someone it makes you seem negative. When you speak positively about someone, it makes you seem positive. Kids have a point when they say "I'm rubber you're glue, whatever you say bounces off of me and sticks to you!" Parents also have a point when they say "If you don't have anything nice to say about someone, don't say anything at all."

7. **Share your passions:** When you are passionate about something it's usually easy to talk about it. Talking about your passions presents you with an opportunity to have interesting conversations. You can share your passion in a very genuine, positive way while enriching your audience with experiences that relate to your passion. Oprah Winfrey said, *"Passion is energy. Feel the power that comes from focusing on what excites you."*

How to Get a Date

Asking someone out on a date is very challenging and nerve-wracking for many men and even more so for many women. There are several ways to make it less challenging and nerve-wracking:

1. **Invest in your appearance and your mental well-being.** Remember that the first point of the relationship framework is to know yourself and invest in yourself so that you can be a better person. Your overall appearance (body language, how you dress, confidence, etc.) is a factor when someone is deciding whether or not to go on a date with you.

2. **Practice having good conversations.** The more you talk to people the more you learn about yourself. For example, when you have a conversation you might learn that there are some things that you enjoy talking about and other things that you are not comfortable talking about. You will also learn that people respond well to some topics and not so well to other topics. You can use that information to have conversations where you focus

on things that you are comfortable talking about that are likely to be well received. For example, you can talk about your passions, positive people who you know or like, or positive experiences that you've had. If you have a good (or great) conversation with someone, there is a good chance that they will be happy to go on a date with you.

3. **Be specific and direct.** People are more likely to accept your invitation if you are clear about what you want or what you want to do. For example, instead of saying "We should hang out sometime" or "Are you doing anything this weekend?" consider one of the following invitations:

   a. *"Let's go to Starbucks for lunch. They have a new Frappuccino I want to try."* This invitation is helpful when you want to keep things simple. For example, if you are just getting to know someone and you don't want to spend time and or money on dinner it's a good idea to start with coffee or something short and sweet. This invitation is also helpful for women who might want to ask a guy out but are not sure if he will say yes. A guy is more likely to say yes to lunch at Starbucks as opposed to dinner at a restaurant.

   b. A more direct invitation can be *"Do you like pasta? I'm asking because I would like to take you to Maggiano's for dinner this weekend."* This invitation makes more sense if you feel that there is a good chance that the person will accept the invitation. The stakes are higher when going out to dinner. Dinner usually suggests that there is a romantic interest or perhaps an interest in a relationship. If you are not interested in a relationship, or you don't have a romantic interest, then you should mention that there are no expectations, and you are just going out as friends. Friends can go out to dinner. As a matter of fact, friends can do anything. It is totally up to you and your friends to decide what is acceptable.

c. Another direct invitation can be *"I want to take you out for your birthday"* or *"I want to take you out to celebrate your graduation/promotion/etc."* If you want to take someone out to celebrate a birthday or milestone, then anything that you think they will enjoy is okay. This includes dinner, movies, plays, concerts, etc. When you specify that you are celebrating an event or a milestone, there is usually no expectation of a romantic relationship. This can be a low-risk opportunity for a woman to ask a man out. If he does not have plans, he is more likely to say yes.

d. A simple, casual invitation can be something along the lines of *"I have a sweet tooth. There's a new ice cream store I would like to take you to. Are you free later on?"* This invitation is helpful when you want to keep things simple. Going out for ice cream is a short and sweet experience. The experience can be unique because many ice cream stores let you sample different flavors of ice cream - which might help you or your date identify a new favorite flavor.

In the examples above I highlighted opportunities for women to ask men out. I realize that some women are traditional and don't like asking men out. That is perfectly okay. If you are one of those women, my suggestion to you is to continue investing in yourself and your appearance, and you will have men asking you out.

Going for a Kiss

Many men play it safe when on dates - which can lead to boring dates. It is generally accepted that if a woman goes out on three or more dates with a man, she is most likely attracted to him on some level. If a man wants to try for a kiss, it is usually safe to try on the third date. This does not mean that she will definitely want to kiss - every woman is different. Some women are ready to kiss on the first date while others may not be ready until the fourth or fifth date or later. The point is that it's okay for a guy to try. It lets the woman know that he desires her in a romantic way. Women like to feel desired – especially if that desire is expressed in a thoughtful, classy way. If a man tries to kiss a woman after they've been out on a few dates, he is taking a small risk. His willingness to take that risk is attractive - especially if she is relaxed and in a good mood.

Note to men: Do not ask if it's okay to kiss – it shows a lack of confidence. Your job is to make sure your date is comfortable and having a good time when you're thinking about kissing her. Do not over analyze the situation. Kisses should be spontaneous – they should not feel planned. They should be the genuine product of a fun interaction between two people who are attracted to each other. You should be responding to the moment, the mood, or the vibe. For example, maybe you were intoxicated by her beauty and could not help yourself – women understand and appreciate that.

If she is not ready to kiss it is perfectly fine. She will not be shocked that you found her attractive and wanted to kiss her. You may even get points because she might be flattered that you have a romantic interest, and you were willing to take a chance. Handle her unwillingness to kiss with grace and calm. You can simply say something along the lines of "My apologies. Kissing you was on my mind." Or you can say "My bad. I was thinking out loud." Then continue the date or conversation as if nothing happened. You took a chance and displayed confidence. If you handle the situation gracefully and respectfully you will probably be presented with another opportunity. This is because how you handle rejection or conflict says a lot about you.

It is important to note that times have changed. It is a traditional concept that men should lead and take the initiative, but sometimes it's okay for a woman to take the initiative. Remember earlier I said that if a woman goes out on a few dates with a man, there is a possible romantic interest. It is also true that if a man takes a woman out on more than one date, it is very likely that he has a romantic interest. This means that the woman can show signs of interest. If the guy is not picking up on the signs of interest, then he may need a little more time. You should recommend this book to him.

Chapter Summary

Many men and women miss out on opportunities because they are afraid of rejection or afraid of making mistakes. Approaching someone of the opposite sex is a very low-risk endeavor. This is especially true in social settings where people want to meet and mingle. If you are uncomfortable approaching people, then don't think of it as an approach. Simply think about initiating a conversation. The more conversations you have, the more comfortable you will be with having conversations. In the future, read the suggestions above more than once so that you become more comfortable with making conversation.

Asking someone out on a date is not easy for many men and women. Sometimes you are afraid to ask someone out because you are worried that they might say no. Keep in mind that there are many people who would love to go out on a date with you. To encourage them to step up remember to invest in yourself and be your best. Also, practice your conversation skills and people will be more likely to approach you and enjoy your company. As you converse with people, you can decide if you want to simply enjoy the conversation or continue the conversation at a later date or on a date.

CHAPTER 9

Good Communication

I am afraid we must make the world honest before we can honestly say to our children that honesty is the best policy.

- George Bernard Shaw

Honesty is Sometimes Not the Best Policy

Honesty is a good policy, but it is sometimes not the best policy. You should be honest about factual information - especially factual information that can be verified. For example, your height, age, weight, marital status, relationship status, employment history, where you live, and whether or not you have kids or examples of factual information that can be verified.

You should be careful when sharing an opinion or a personal point of view. You probably do this without realizing it. For example, if you don't like someone because you feel that they are boring, it is honest to say "I don't like you because I think you're boring." Is that the best thing to say? Absolutely not. It's better to say something along the lines of "Thanks for sharing your feelings. I would like us to be friends." This response is an example of good communication. Notice that it is truthful, and it gets the point across. Good communication is more important than honesty because your honest opinion might be controversial or might cause the other person to be defensive.

Parents and or teachers often tell kids that honesty is the best policy. Ironically, kids know that they can't always be honest with their parents or teachers because they might be punished as a result. For example, if a kid tells their parent that they don't like their dinner it might cause the parent to chastise them or threaten not to feed them. Some parents would say things like "Stop complaining! You should be glad to have food to eat." Or they might say something along the lines of "You are so ungrateful! There are many kids who would feel lucky to have food to eat." Usually strict or controlling parents react this way.

On the flip side, sometimes parents (or adults in general) are not honest with children because they don't feel that children can handle the truth. Or perhaps they don't want to be discouraging. There are easy examples that involve Santa, the Tooth Fairy, and the Easter Bunny, but I won't use those examples because I like those characters. I'll use a personal example.

I visited one of my college buddies and spent a few days with his family. He has a great wife and three adorable kids. His kids are eight years old, five years old, and four years old. I got up for breakfast one morning, and the kids offered to make me pancakes. I was impressed that they knew how to make pancakes, so I said "Sure. I like pancakes". It turns out that I did not like their pancakes - they tasted terrible. When they asked me if I liked the pancakes, I paused before answering. I wanted to reply *"No. I don't like these pancakes. Why do your parents let you make pancakes?"* That reply, however, might have been discouraging. So I thought for a second maybe I should say *"Yes. They're good."* But I did not want to lie and encourage them to continue making bad pancakes. So I decided that the best response was *"I like the fact that you all made pancakes. You guys are great kids."* Then I changed the subject.

I make a distinction between being honest and communicating well because people sometimes confuse their personal opinion with honesty. When you state your personal opinion as if it is a fact, it can cause problems in your relationships (friendship, dating, or marriage). For example, if you don't like someone's cooking, that does not mean that they can't cook, or that they are a bad cook. Or, if you feel that someone is being mean to you or being selfish, that does not mean that they are a mean or selfish person. You can communicate how you feel without making it seem like a personal attack or a broad generalization. For example, instead of saying "You're a mean person." Or "You're a selfish person." You can say something along the lines of "I feel that you are mean to me." Or "I feel that you are being selfish right now."

Honest Compliments

You may sometimes feel that you are honest when you compliment someone. For example, if you feel that someone has nice arms or nice legs it makes sense to tell them that they have nice arms or legs. The problem here is that your honest compliment may cause the person to feel uncomfortable. This usually happens if your timing or delivery is bad. Also, they might feel uncomfortable if they are not attracted to you. Look and listen for signs of interest before complimenting someone's looks. Compliments often do not generate romantic interest. Romantic interest often happens before you say anything. This is because your body language and appearance determine whether or not someone is attracted to you.

Sometimes it is best to compliment someone's accomplishments. For example, if someone is a musician or a performer and you enjoyed watching them perform let them know. Or if you feel that someone did a great job of color coordinating their outfit let them know that. People are more receptive to compliments that relate to their accomplishments.

Truth, Lies, and Good Communication

Good communication is a good alternative to lies and risky truth telling. A good communicator seldom feels a need to lie because he or she can say what needs to be said without hurting someone's feelings. Consider the following scenario: Someone likes you romantically but you don't like them because you are not attracted to them. Perhaps you don't like their appearance - their style, their vibe, or their body type. Perhaps you are not sure why you don't like them. The important thing is that the attraction is not mutual.

If the attraction is not mutual, it is honest, but ill-advised, to say that you are not attracted to them. Your honesty in this situation may be hurtful. You don't want to hurt anyone's feelings if you can avoid doing so. This is especially important if the person who likes you has been nice to you. In these types of scenarios many men and women say that they are dating someone or that they are taking a break from dating. Sometimes this is not true, but it is totally understandable because it is done to spare the person's feelings.

When initially turning someone down a better response would be a simple, respectful, and truthful statement. "I" statements usually help you accomplish this goal. Consider the following "I" statements:

a. *"Thank you, but I'm not interested."* This response may work if you don't know the person or if you wish to keep things short and sweet. It's simple and direct. If you can say it with a smile, that may help soften the rejection. A nice smile goes a long way.

b. *"Thank you for letting me know, but I don't see you that way."* Or *"Thanks but I'm not into you like that."* These types of statements may work if you know the person but you don't know them very well. Note that there is a subtle suggestion that you are not into them at the moment. You may feel different about them at another time.

c. *"Thank you for sharing how you feel. I want us to be friends. Are you okay with us being friends?"* This response is helpful if you like the person as a friend but you are not sure if you should date them. Also, notice how this response puts the ball in the other person's court. They now have a chance to accept or reject you. If they are okay with being friends, and you have a good friendship, then you will have a good foundation for dating or courting. Remember the saying *"Friendship leads to love, but love never leads to friendship"* - Lord Byron.

Nice Guy Communication

Nice guys sometimes finish last because they are afraid to say the wrong thing or suggest the wrong thing. For example, some guys don't plan dates or activities. Instead, they ask the woman "What do you want to do?" Many women find this question annoying - especially if the guy asked them out. Women like men with a plan. A man should have a plan A, a plan B, and a plan C. Several plans are a good idea because if the woman does not like the first plan, the man can offer an alternative plan.

Communication can be tough sometimes but the more you practice, the easier it gets. Chapter 8 offers many simple solutions to help you practice having conversations. For example, you can practice politely sharing your opinions in safe settings - among friends or family. When you practice sharing your opinions, you will have an easier time communicating your opinions.

Chapter Summary

One of the most important ways to be a better person is to communicate well. If you see a list of men's wants or women's wants that contains "honesty," without any clarification, you should ignore it. Honesty is a good policy, but it is sometimes not the best policy. Your honest opinion can be hurtful to some. Or it can get you in trouble. To avoid problems, you should think of the best way to express your opinions or concerns. Your goal should be to communicate well and not offend.

Communication is a key component of the relationship framework. For example, when you know yourself you should know how you communicate and how well you communicate. You should be aware of how you are perceived when you communicate. There is a great book about how you are perceived entitled *No One Understands You and What to Do About it*. The author, Heidi Halvorson, addresses many key components related to how you communicate, and how you are perceived as a result.

When you understand and appreciate others, you should try to understand how they communicate. Men and women often have different communication styles. For example, men tend to communicate directly with each other - hints are kept to a minimum. Women, on the other hand, are more likely to hint at what they want. This is one of the reasons women sometimes don't want men to be themselves. When men don't get the hint, they are being themselves. Also, when men don't listen well, they are being themselves. Listening well is a superpower for many men - it doesn't happen easily. To be better persons, men and women should listen well.

CHAPTER 10

Spirituality and Self

You were taught, with regard to your former way of life, to put off your old self, which is being corrupted by its deceitful desires; to be made new in the attitude of your minds; and to put on the new self, created to be like God in true righteousness and holiness.

- Ephesians 4:22-24 (NIV) [26]

Can you be Spiritual and Be Yourself?

It is sometimes odd when a religious person says "Be yourself." Most religions and belief systems discourage the unguided individuality that is often exhibited by the "be yourself" mindset. The four largest religions in the world - Christianity, Islam, Hinduism, and Buddhism - encourage their believers to be better. For example, Christians are encouraged to be like Jesus. According to the Bible, *"In your relationships with one another, have the same mindset as Christ Jesus." (Philippians 2:5 NIV)*. These factors present us with the question "Can you be spiritual and be yourself?" Let's take a look at some specific challenges related to being yourself - from a spiritual [Christian] perspective.

Peter's Denial of Christ

I am familiar with Biblical guidelines regarding behavior and self because I am a Christian. The story of Peter's denial of Christ - which is detailed in the Gospels of Matthew, Mark, Luke, and John - illustrates one of the reasons religions, in general, do not want their adherents to be themselves. For my readers who are not Christian, I think you will see the point once we review the story.

In the Gospel according to Matthew, Jesus had a meeting with his disciples and told them "This very night you will all fall away on account of me, for it is written: 'I will strike the shepherd, and the sheep of the flock will be scattered.' " (Matthew 26:31 NIV). Jesus was referring to the fact that he would be arrested that night, and his disciples would abandon him.

Peter, one of Jesus's disciples, replied, "Even if all fall away on account of you, I never will." (Verse 33). Peter was basically saying that he would never abandon Jesus.

Jesus then told Peter, "This very night, before the rooster crows, you will disown me three times." (Verse 34).

Peter then declared, "Even if I have to die with you, I will never disown you." And all the other disciples said the same (verse 35).

Later in the day, Jesus went to a place called Gethsemane to pray for strength because he knew that he would be betrayed and arrested that night. He took Peter and a few other disciples with him and said to them, "My soul is overwhelmed with sorrow to the point of death. Stay here and keep watch with me." (Verse 38). Jesus then went away and came back to find Peter and the other disciples sleeping. He then said to them, "Couldn't you men keep watch with me for one hour? Watch and pray so that you will not fall into temptation. The spirit is willing, but the flesh is weak." (Verse 41). Jesus wanted Peter and the disciples to pray for strength because they were about to be tested.

As predicted, when Jesus was arrested the disciples abandoned him because they feared for their safety. Peter, on the other hand, did not totally abandon Jesus. He followed from a distance to see the outcome of Jesus' arrest. While Peter was observing Jesus (from a distance) different people, on three occasions, identified him as one of Jesus' disciples. Each time Peter denied being one of the disciples. His last denial included cursing and swearing. Immediately after Peter's third denial, the rooster crowed. Peter then remembered Jesus' prediction that he would deny him three times before the rooster crowed.

Prayer and Strength

Why did the disciples abandon Jesus when he was arrested? They said that they would not abandon him yet they abandoned him the same night. Why did Peter deny Jesus three times after Jesus warned him that he would deny him three times? The answer is simple - they were weak and afraid. They feared for their safety. That is why Jesus told them to pray. He wanted them to pray for strength.

In your natural state, you are sometimes weak and afraid. Your fears and weaknesses are the causes for many of your shortcomings. Here are some common fears:

- Fear of doing what is right

- Fear of speaking out against injustice

- Fear of communicating your concerns, likes, or dislikes

- Fear of approaching a stranger or initiating conversation with a stranger

- Fear of trusting or being vulnerable

- Fear of having faith and trusting God

Fear and weakness are very common human traits, which is why Peter was being himself when he denied Jesus. The disciples were also themselves when they abandoned Jesus after his arrest. You are yourself when you are afraid or when you give in to temptation. The Bible says that "the flesh is weak." As a result, Christians are encouraged to pray regularly for strength to avoid giving in to temptation. If someone has not prayed for strength, you may not want them to be themselves.

Prayer and meditation have significant benefits. From a spiritual perspective, prayer is a reminder that you have limits - physically and mentally. It is a reminder that there are many things that you don't understand and will never understand. Prayer also has scientifically-supported benefits.[27] For example, prayer can improve your self-control, make you nicer, make you more forgiving, increase your sense of trust, and offset the negative health consequences of stress. Prayer can help you become a better person - which is why many religions encourage their believers to pray regularly.

Chapter Summary

Most major religions and belief systems have a deity or supreme being. That supreme being knows that many men and women are frail, limited, and susceptible to temptation. Even good men and women have a bad side. If unchecked, these men and women would become victims of their bad selves. This is why the Christian Bible states that *"The heart is deceitful above all things, and desperately wicked: who can know it?"* Jeremiah 17:9 (KJV). To avoid succumbing to their bad side and giving in to temptation, believers are often encouraged to pray and meditate.

Prayer and meditation benefit your mind and body in many ways. [25] Remarkably, some of the common prayer and meditation positions are similar to yoga. Your mind and body have great potential. As a result, you can do great things. The inspired founders of most belief systems are acutely aware of your potential for greatness. These founders encourage you to improve physically, mentally, and spiritually. As you improve spiritually you set the foundation for a good spiritual connection with someone.

Conclusion

Twenty years from now you will be more disappointed by the things you didn't do than by the ones you did do. So throw off the bowlines. Sail away from the safe harbor. Catch the trade winds in your sail. Explore. Dream. Discover.

- Mark Twain

Thank You

This book was written to disrupt the "be yourself" mindset and encourage you to be a better person. We looked at when to be yourself and when not to be yourself. You know not to fall into the trap of thinking that there are only two choices – 1) be yourself or 2) pretend to be someone else. This book presented a third option – 3) be a better person. To help you become a better person this book offered a **relationship framework** with three steps:

1. Know yourself and invest in yourself so that you can be a better person.
2. Understand and appreciate the needs and perspectives of others (especially the opposite sex).
3. Think of the best interaction or relationship that makes sense for you and the other person.

After reading this book, you should know yourself a little better. Also, you should understand and appreciate the needs and perspectives of others (especially the opposite sex). We looked at men's wants and women's wants. We also looked at sex appeal and swag and discussed the importance of both. We also looked at why men don't approach and offered tested remedies to avoid approach anxiety and communicate well.

I appreciate your interest and support and thank you for reading this book. Please share the insights that you benefited from with others. Remember that "Happiness is not only about finding the right person it is also about BEING the right person." My wish is for you to be the right person - a more knowledgeable person - a better person.

Bibliography

[1] D W Sue, P Arredondo, and R J McDavis, "Multicultural counseling competencies and standards: a call to the profession," *Journal of Counseling & Development*, vol. 70, pp. 477-486, 1992.

[2] Bryan Roche, "10 Ways to Improve Your Brain Health," *Psychology Today*, July 2014.

[3] Lea Winerman, "Thin Slices of Life," *American Psychological Association*.

[4] Dana Dovey, "Study: Men Think Smart Women Are Sexy, They Just Wouldn't Date One," *Medical Daily*, October 2015.

[5] Theresa E DiDonato, "Do Nice Guys Really Finish Last? When warm and kind faces off against bold and sexy," *Psychology Today*, May 2014.

[6] Gigi Engle. (2015, April) 5 Scientific Reasons Why Women Just Won't Go For The Nice Guys.

[7] Raymond Fisman, Sethi Iyengar Sheena, Emir Kamenica, and Itamar Simonson, *Gender Differences in Mate Selection: Evidence from a Speed Dating Experiment*. New York: Columbia University: Academic Commons, 2006.

[8] Paula Mejia. (2014, July) Study Finds That Men Like Nice

Women, But Not the Other Way Around.

[9] Jeannie Assimos, "First Dates: Who Should Pay.and Why,"
    EHarmony Blog RSS, July 2014.

[10] Susan Krauss Whitbourne, "5 Tips for Tough Conversations
    With Your Partner," *Psychology Today*, June 2014.

[11] Bruna Martinuzzi. Open Forum.

[12] Heidi Grant Halvorson, *No One Understands You and What to
    Do about It*. Boston, MA: Harvard Business Review Press, 2015.

[13] D J Schneider, *The psychology of stereotyping*. New York, NY:
    Guilford Press, 2005.

[14] Gary D Chapman, *The 5 Love Languages: The Secret to Love
    that Lasts*, Reprint edition ed. Chicago, IL: Northfield
    Publishing, 2015.

[15] Laura E. Berk, *Development through the Lifespan. 4th ed.*
    Boston, MA: Allyn and Bacon, 2007.

[16] Nadine Harris. (2014, September) How Childhood Trauma
    Affects Health across a Lifetime.

[17] P Heaven and J Ciarrochi, "Parental styles, gender and the
    development of hope and self-esteem," *European Journal Of
    Personality*, vol. 22, no. 8, pp. 707-724, 2008.

[18] Sigmund Freud, *Group Psychology and the Analysis of the Ego*.
    New York: Norton, 1975.

[19] Denver Nicks, "Hitting Your Kids Is Legal in All 50 States," *Time*,

September 2014.

[20] RAINN. Rape, Abuse and Incest National Network. [Online]. https://rainn.org/

[21] Lisa Jones, "The Top 20 Traits Women Want in a Man," *Men's Health*, March 2015.

[22] Ian Kerner. (2008, January) Today Health & Wellness. [Online]. http://www.today.com/health

[23] Dean M Busby, Jason S Carroll, and Brian J Willoughby, "Compatibility or restraint? The effects of sexual timing on marriage relationships," *Journal of Family Psychology*, vol. 24, no. 6, pp. 766-774, December 2010.

[24] Ronald E Riggio, "The 4 Key Elements of Sex Appeal," *Psychology Today*, February 2016.

[25] Susan Kuchinskas. Meditation Health Benefits and Stress Reduction.

[26] The Holy Bible, *The Holy Bible: New International Version, Containing the Old Testament and the New Testament*. Grand Rapids, MI: Zondervan Bible Publishers, 1978.

[27] Clay Routledge, "5 Scientifically Supported Benefits of Prayer," *Psychology Today*, February 2016.

[28] Sigmund Freud and James Strachey, *The Ego and the Id*. New York: Norton, 1962.

[29] Robert B. Cialdini, *Influence: The Psychology of Persuasion. Rev. Ed.* New York: Collins, 2007.

[30] A J Cuddy, M Kohut, and J Neffinger, "Connect, Then Lead," *Harvard Business Review*, July 2013.

[31] Robert Greene and Joost Elffers, *The 48 Laws of Power*. New York: Penguin Books, 2000.

[32] Emanuella Grinberg. (2011, November) Effects of Physical Discipline Linger for Adults.

[33] Hinduism. (2016, February) Hinduism. [Online]. https://en.wikipedia.org/wiki/Hinduism

[34] Talal Itani, *Quran English Translation. Clear, Easy to Read, in Modern English*.

[35] Leil Lowndes, *How to Talk to Anyone 92 Little Tricks for Big Success in Relationships*. Chicago, IL: Contemporary Books, 2003.

[36] Aaron Mays, "Why Nice Guys Don't Always Make It to the Top," *Stanford Graduate School of Business*, October 2011.

[37] C Munsey, "Childhood Personality Can Predict Adult Behavior," *American Psychological Association*, February 2006.

[38] NPR. (2014, December) Some Early Childhood Experiences Shape Adult Life, But Which Ones?

[39] Lora E Park, Ariana F Young, and Paul W Eastwick, "(Psychological) Distance Makes the Heart Grow Fonder: Effects of Psychological Distance and Relative Intelligence on Men's Attraction to Women," *Personality and Social Psychology Bulletin*, vol. 41, no. 11, pp. 1459–1473, 2015.

[40] Allan Pease and Barbara Pease, *The Definitive Book of Body Language*. New York: Bantam Books, 2006.

[41] Joe Navarro and Marvin Karlins, *What Every BODY Is Saying: An Ex-FBI Agent's Guide to Speed-reading People*. New York, NY: Collins Living, 2008.

[42] Jason Powers, "Doing These Two Things Will Boost Your Well-Being," *Psychology Today*, September 2015.

[43] Jessica Samakow. (2014, September) What Science Says About Using Physical Force To Punish A Child.

[44] P B Smith, R Fischer, V L Vignoles, and M H Bond, *Understanding Social Psychology Across Cultures: Engaging with Others in a Changing World*. Los Angeles, CA: Sage Publications, 2003.

[45] Abdullah Yusuf Ali, *The Holy Qurán*. Ware, Hertfordshire: Wordsworth Editions, 2000.

[46] Bill Hendrick. (2010, December) WebMD Health News. [Online]. http://www.webmd.com

[47] Anatta. Wikipedia. [Online]. https://en.wikipedia.org/wiki/Anatta

Special Thanks

This was an incredibly fun book to write. As a single male, an avid reader, a psychology student, and someone who wants to improve, I enjoyed reading and researching so that I could provide you with informative, interesting content.

I am grateful to my mom for her consistent love and support. I am also grateful to my brother Godfrey for proofreading this book and providing valuable insight. I want to say a special thank you to my friends for providing feedback and sharing many interesting experiences. Lastly, I thank you, the reader for your support and interest in this book. I wish you the very best in your interactions and relationships.

Feedback

Feel free to provide feedback on Amazon.com. If you have critical feedback, please use the book's website - it is easier for me to track feedback entered on the book's website.

This book's website: www.dbybook.com

David Ross' website: www.davidrossblog.com

About David Ross

David Ross is a blogger and a fan of good discussions. He has a bachelor's degree in Mathematics, a master's degree in Psychology, and is currently a Ph.D. student at the Chicago School of Professional Psychology. His area of focus is International Psychology. David is also an active member of the American Psychological Association and the American Psychological Association of Graduate Students

David was born in Brooklyn, New York and lives in Atlanta, Georgia. He enjoys playing tennis, swimming, home improvement projects, and DJing. To contact David Ross feel free to use the information below:

Website: www.davidrossblog.com

About David Ross